" E G O - O L O G Y "

YESTERDAY,

TODAY,

AND

TOMORROW

BY

VICTOR R. HARRIS

PUBLISHED BY:

V.R.H. PRODUCTIONS, INC.
Washington, D.C.

Rotcivsirrah0925@gmail.com

DEDICATION

This book is Dedicated to all women and men who are striving to achieve a high moral standard in life and those who are endeavoring to reach their higher self. Thus, their connection to GOD.
This book is, also, Dedicated to the striving laborer and those struggling to get above the level of poverty. To the seeker of truth and understanding.
This book is, also, Dedicated to the members of V.R.H. Productions Incorporated and A.G.E. Incorporated and to all striving students, especially Federal City College (which became the University Of the District of Columbia), Coppin State College, Morgan State University, and the Community College of Baltimore from which I have attended classes. To all those who help mankind evolve, improve, to make it fit for the Kingdom of God.

E G O - O L O G Y

INTRODUCTION

Ego-ology is the science of the development, establishment, and usage of the Ego/self character of women and men. It is, also, the image or reflection of the purpose and character of groups and organizations. This includes maintaining such an Ego or character. To generalize the term further you could even include the image of animals, and any other descriptive forms of life, even death can have an ego. It's funny, though, how other forms of life maintain their order yet man has a problem in keeping whatever his purpose is straight.

This science applies various common principles to define the nature of an entity, whether it be an individual or a group. And, then as the individual or group develops to perform its function in life it is predestined to accomplish certain feats or tasks and to maintain its behavior. These are the norms of the ego or image and being of an entity in the ego's task or goal.

For example, all students currently taking up Sociology, and that's their Major in college, will all be educated and developed, basically, the same way. They all will go into the work field exercising the principles they have learned. If they did anything other than that we would have to conclude that they have erred.

Ego-olgy takes into consideration the limitations or boundaries of the entity. To do so keeps it defined. To not do so means to err.

Some people have claimed that "man knows no boundaries." However, such a statement has failed to respect the character of man. This slick quote seems to be speaking of a God man both Good and Evil. For, without boundaries you would surely exercise in both. Or it could be speaking of the SuperEgo or some eternal aspect of man. Even still, freedom requires responsibility or you would interfere with the freedom of others. Then how long would one be free, especially if your infringement is offensive?

Tell me, can a thing be blessed and cursed at the same time? Does oil and water mix? Even our world has defined God as being all good. And God man as the image of God. Evil is said to be of the Devil. Then the Ego has boundaries. And it's also subject to definition.

In our modern day society and throughout history many have deviated, regressed, or have sought to realign the Ego and progress it to its natural fulfillment and then help it to discover its being divested of the True Ego they were or should have been. Thus, Ego-ology means and seeks to realign the Ego and progress it to its natural fulfillment and then help it to discover its superego. Endeavoring to pursue and reach the SuperEgo can be before but mainly will be after the Ego task or goal has been completed. His purpose in life then has been fulfilled. Or at least his first vocation.

The study of Ego-ology and the purpose of this book is to encourage people of this AGE to look closely at the True Ego of an entity, as the Ego should be: be it person, place, or thing (this first book is limited to people) it has an ego. Yet, many today look past the True purpose of an Ego Entity and end up elsewhere in thought and behavior. Even a hammer wasn't designed to screw.

By observing the Ego Entity we can see those who deviate from their True form, from the character they are supposed to portray. The social scientist is expected to perform the duties of such. If a clergyman is constantly intoxicated at the pew or dating six different Deaconesses, we can easily determine that this is not in line with the image of a minister.

Once we determine the flaws in character we can work towards improving the True Ego of the entity. Then we can bring it back to its true design. Of course, that's not as easy as it may sound. But it's worth the effort.

If I am not what I say I am, then I am not. If people profess one thing and do another they are not the thing that they proclaim to be. They are either being hypocritical or as dead to the True Ego Entity. They could also be lost, blind, false, confused or sick. Or they simply haven't discovered how to handle the pressures associated with the Ego task so they avoid it.

Even in a person's name you can find a definition of character, especially Islamic names. For instance, a man named Amin (which means trustworthy) you wouldn't expect to be short changing the cash register or juggling the inventory sheet to steal supplies. Or Joshua (a jewish name meaning one of God) to be conjuring up the Devil in some satanic cult.

Even when you look at persons born in certain families like the Kennedys and the Mitchel Family, (out of Baltimore), which are political families, you wouldn't expect them to be Drug lords. The image of their family is political

Organizations function from the same ideology. They describe themselves and that's what you expect. You wouldn't expect the Klu-Klux- Klan to be dating blacks. Or the New Shiloh Baptist Church selling ponography.. Their image would be flawed and severed if contrary activity was a part of them.

Therefore, to know one's name or one's purpose or True Ego is enough to show what that person should be doing. Of course, you may claim the statement that no one's perfect. I don't think you need to be perfect to fit these natural common descriptions.

So the goal of Ego-ology is to study the Ego Entity or Ego, determine what kind it is and where it is in it's development or in relation to its goal or manifestation. If the Ego is afield, then the study would seek to determine how far it is and how to return it to its proper place.

This book is designed to show what the Ego is, some of the different types of Egos, How to adapt to and/or shun different Egos. And how to help your Ego and that of others to become what you and they should be. It, also, helps you to know when a person is straying from their True Ego or Ego task and makes suggestions on what you can do to bring the Ego back into proper perspective.

The book concludes by showing you the Id, Ego, and SuperEgo and how they are related to the SubConscious, Conscious, and SuperConsciousness. Then it links it all to the internal, external, and Universal worlds. These terms may not have the exact meaning as they were coined earlier by Sigmund Frued.

The last chapter speaks on Ego-ology and the future. How this science can be applied to strengthening relationships and supporting the growth and development of all our true goals and ambitions.

Remember to keep in mind that the author is being philosophical yet using very common truths and common sense. The book, nevertheless, is very interesting. Read it!
very common truths and common sense.

There is a scripture in the Holy Bible that says " stay in the work wherein you were called." That means that once life has placed you in what you are to do you needn't chase after other causes. You pray for them and allow God to bring into existence that which will solve the new problem. If you just leap at other causes you may cause your own to falter or lack. You can also block those persons that may already exist to solve that problem. Find what's yours and respect what others may have to do in life. They are just as important as you. We need each other.

E G O - O L O G Y

TABLE OF CONTENTS

PART I - EGO-DESCRIPTIONS

TABLE OF CONTENTS
(Continued)

TABLE OF CONTENTS
(Continued)

Blank Page

PART I.

EGO - DESCRIPTIONS

*

*

*

*

*

*

*

EGO, CHARACTER, AND SELF ESTEEM

Contentment is a form of consenting
which doesn't encourage anything,
but implies satisfaction

The mind does not act from a thought it doesn't have
and satisfaction is fulfillment

Therefore, if you know you have not reached your goal
and all possibilities of doing so are not dead,
then you must ignite the mind to pursue

****

Truth is measurable so that we can all see and know it

****

The work of life belongs to the Ego

****

It's somebody's business to do everything

CHAPTER I.

THE EGO, CHARACTER, AND SELF ESTEEM

THE EGO

The Ego is that entity, that portion or aspect of the being that says, " I Am That I Am." Yet, this Ego doesn't have to be all of man, he has a SuperEgo too. What that Ego Entity becomes, The I Am such as, I Am an Architect or I Am a Doctor, defines it.

This I Am or Ego is the basis of the character of man. I will stick to the image of man for this chapter because the subject of the Ego of groups and organizations will be discussed later along with a chapter on the Id, Ego, and SuperEgo.

Since there can be more than one Ego, in the theory of Ego-ology, the Multiple Ego must be understood as well. The Multiple Ego would say "I am a Singer and a Philosopher. Two distinct sets of norms will be present. This subject will be covered later as well.

I simply wanted to, somewhat, introduce our definition of the Ego not as a mere role that one plays, but a being that must perform and accomplish set goals in life. I call these goals "Ego Goals." The objectives that he uses as steps towards achieving these Ego Goals I call " Ego Objectives." The "Ego Task" is the work that the Ego has. And his affiliates that help him reach his goals or who just support the Ego I call the "Ego Circle."

Character

According to Huffman, Vernoy,and Vernoy in "Psychology In Action." (1994) (484-490) they explain " In the type, trial, and psychoanalytic approaches...personality is seen as an abstract internal part of each individual that may or may not be related to external behavior.

From the learning perspective the term "personality " is used as a concrete, external label for the sum total of an individual's behavior. Personality is assessed from the outside by measuring observable behaviors, such as public speaking or attending parties."

Character can have more than one trait or aspect of itself. Such as happy and alert, intelligent and wanting. However, each part of the terms of description must somehow be compatible and not contradictory, like, happy and sad, witty and stupid won't get it either. At least not at the same time.

Character can also be descriptive of the role that a person plays and that of the son's real face. Character as a role is (for the purposes of Ego-ology) also called the Ego Image. Character is the essence of the behavior of a person. It's like a road map to expectations of the Ego Entity. Character defines, prescribes, what the character would be and should be.

Of course, character is also defined by an Ego Entity's status, reputation, moral belief and its general attitude in his affairs. His way of doing things. And in Ego-ology we seek to study character to determine the Ego and vice-versa, we study the Ego to determine character.

Remember that the Ego Entity's character is the nexus to the True Ego. Especially as is reflected in his Ego Task.

Self Esteem

Self Esteem is the realization of the Ego with its Ego Image in self acceptance and approval. It is the belief in and recognition of the Ego Image in a most elated manner. It's self satisfaction, pride and contentment. It's a climatic peak-an optimum.

Self Esteem is normally triggered by external factors that spark internal reaction. Sometimes when people acknowledge some achievement of the Ego Entity self esteem is attained.

Self Esteem can also be treacherously manipulated by deceit. Simply because someone is aware of the Ego Entity's wishes for accomplishment or his desires to hear nice things regarding his Ego. They call it being "stroked." Of course, there are negative strokes and positive strokes.

Negative strokes are more in line to mellifluously build you up to let you down or to make you believe you have victoriously obtained something that you are far short of achieving. And positive strokes, on the other hand, are respectfully designed to encourage a person's performance. And to gender incentive to maintain good self esteem to accomplish Ego objectives and the Ego task.

Carl Rogers (1902-1987) felt that the most vital aspect of the personality was the self. The self being the "I" or me that one defines himself as. Humanistic psychologists like him today call this the Self-Concept.

According to Rogers, the feelings each of us has about ourselves, either good or bad, is self esteem. Also, that your mental health is directly related to the degree of congruence between your self concept and life experiences. If your self concept is reasonably consistent and overlaps with actual life experiences the self is said to be congruent and the person is "Well adjusted." The reverse is true when there is little overlap and incongruity.

Also unconditional positive regard Rogers term for how we should behave toward someone to increase his or her self esteem, positive behavior shown toward a person with no contingencies attached (according to "Psychology In Action."

Our point is that self esteem is related to truth, therefore, it isn't weighed independent of a man's true purpose and his Ego task.

The Ego task is the work designed to accomplish Ego objectives towards the Ego Goal. Without the attainments of the Ego Objectives through his works there could be no voice or reflection or act by which the Ego can declare itself. For instance, to paint (the Ego task) is the work that helps the Ego Entity; the painter (the Ego Objective). But, to be the great Painter (The Ego Goal) the Ego Entity must be satisfied beyond his own self acceptance. He must sell the Masterpiece, become the talk of the town, and/or mentioned in the books and archives.

The Ego Entity can tell that he is not being stroked by others just to help his self esteem. If someone says, "that song you wrote is the most beautiful song I have ever heard," yet won't spend one dime to buy it, you can easily take it that it's worth isn't that much to that person. Or someone visits your restaurant and says, "your food is great " yet never eats a meal, there is no proof or substance to validate the claim.

As long as the Ego Entity has a task it can be alive. But when the Ego Entity has no objective he is more or less a dead Ego. It does nothing. Even if it has another activity. To the cause of that Ego Entity he has nothing else to accomplish. He can, however, start another cause. And too, each Ego Objective is like building blocks. Therefore, he can't afford to miss not one.

If the Ego Entity needs self esteem he should receive it whenever he accomplishes any feats or reaches an objective. I say, if he needs self esteem because some Ego Entities could care less. They practise being concerned about others and helping their plight. However, it's hard for the average person not to smile when he has accomplished something or feel relieved when an Ego Objective has been reached.

Erikson pointed out the significance of "Generativity" to adult development. That need to accomplish something with one's life. And there are more than 20,000 Job categories in the dictionary of Occupational Titles.

In Barbara Shers and Barbara Smith's book, " I Could Do Anything " on page (3) they comment as such: "...Einstein needed to formulate theories of physics, Harriet Tubman needed to guide people to freedom, and you need to follow your original vision. As Vartan Gregorian said, " The Universe is not going to see someone like you again in the entire history of creation. Each of us are one of a kind. Every person has a completely original way of looking at the world, and originality always needs to express itself.

...one reason why it's so hard to know what we want is that we have so many options... It's a tribute to the success of our culture that so many of us have the freedom to search for our own life's work."

In Ego-ology we, therefore, seek to maintain self esteem in our accomplishments of our Ego Objectives. We, also, seek to reward those who achieve those objectives to help reinforce positive behavior and keep the Ego Entity motivated towards obtaining other objectives and their Ego Goal.

We also note that the need to survive can sometimes cause the Ego Entity to abandon his current objectives so that he can equip himself with essentials for the task or difficulties he must face forthcoming. Which brings us to Abraham H. Maslow (1954-1970) quoting from " Motivation and Personality, 2d ed. (New York: Harper & Brothers, 1970)

" Abraham Maslow developed the Hierarchy of Needs, a theory of Motivation that arranges five universal needs in order of priority: (1) physiological needs for food, water, etc. (2) safety for physical and psychological security, (3) belongingness needs for love and inclusion; (40) esteem needs for self respect, and (5) self actualization needs to reach one's potential.

SELF ACTUALIZATION
(Realization)
To find self-fulfillment
and realize one's potential

ESTEEM
To achieve, be competent,
gain approval, and excel

BELONGINGNESS
To affiliate with others, be accepted
and give and receive attention

SAFETY
To feel secure and safe, to seek
pleasure and avoid pain

PHYSIOLOGICAL
Hunger, thirst, and maintenance of
internal state of body

Once freed from the lower needs humans are drawn to satisfy needs that will help them grow and develop." (Geller, 1982, Neher, 1991; Williams and Page, 1989) People sometimes seek to satisfy higher level needs even when one's lower needs aren't met.

It is imperative that the Ego Entity maintain focus on his real Ego Objectives despite the fact that he may or has deviated from his task. In Ego-ology we want to make sure that the Ego Entity is brought back to his path by himself or members of his Ego circle. They too must keep a watchful eye on the Ego Entity.

In " Managing Human Resources " by Sherman & Bohlander (9th ed.) they list five stages of career development.

STAGES OF CAREER DEVELOPMENT

STAGE 1: Preparation for Work

Typical Age Range: 0 - 25

Major Tasks: Development occupational self image, assess alternative occupations, develop initial occu-pational choice, pursue necessary education

STAGE 2: Organizational Entry

Typical Age Range: 18 - 25

Major Tasks: Obtain job offer(s) from desired organization(s), select appropriate job based on accurate data

STAGE 3: Early Career

Typical Age Range: 25 -40

Major Tasks: Learn job, learn organizational rules and norms, fit into chosen occupation and organization, in-crease competence, pursue goals.

STAGE 4: MidCareer

Typical Age Range: 40 - 55

Major Tasks: Reappraise early career and early adulthood, re-
                        affirm or modify goals, make choices appropriate
                        to middle adult years, remain productive in work.

STAGE 5: Late Career

Typical Age Range: 55 - Retirement

Major Tasks: Remain productive in work, maintain self-esteem,
                        prepare for effective retirement.

    From Career Management, by
        J.H. Greenhaus

Each person must earnestly seek to discover exactly what he needs to do as a purpose or goal in life. A man's purpose comes with self realization. Therefore, an Ego Entity must dig deep into himself to determine his vocation. Once he has concluded what his vocation is he must then learn all of the essential components for his task. That's when his Ego Circle becomes helpful to him. How do you develop your circle?

In the book " I Could Do Anything " M's Sher and Smith point out some helpful suggestions on finding the Ego Task or Goal.
On page (163):

1.   THINK LIKE A HUNTER

Do you want to be a Journalist? Find out where they go after work. Give it a little thought and you'll know where your people hang out. Go find them. Be outspoken. Tell the people you meet about your interests. Even if they are not the right people. After all, they might point you in the right direction

2.   SEND UP A FLARE

Personal ads are too good to be used only for the romance market. Place an ad saying "Is anyone interested in talking over coffee about trekking across antarctica? Call me."

3.   READ JOURNALS LEFT BY SOMEONE WHO
KNEW THE TERRITORY

You're different from your family, but someone out there who was just like you had written a book. Find it, and paste quotes all over your house so you never forget who you are.

4.   DO ANYTHING

Avoid tunnel vision. Look for offbeat things to do. Accompany your friends when they go places you might not otherwise go. As many people find their tribe through serendipity as through design.

AT PAGE (119) THEY STATE:

...Nature will come halfway and help you. What do I mean by nature? I mean the materials you work with. Your materials might be numbers or sounds or words or wood or gravity or weather or physics. If you're working with people, your material is human nature.

If you find yourself indecisive you have a burden to overcome. Choose your work and your affiliates and get on with your life or you may find yourself wasting away. And once you find your cause keep focus or you may become lost from your true Ego and its purpose. Being blinded by that you may end up with a false Ego. Where that may carry the Entity (you) God only knows.

THE LOST, BLIND, AND FALSE EGO

The Lost Knows Not
The Blind Sees Not
The False Is Not

****

Never Deny The Truth
For By Doing So
You Become Blinded To It

****

How Can We Know
A Lie?
For It Is Not

****

Can One That's Down Fall?

****

Never Consent To That Which Will
Take You Astray
Even A Little Bit Away
Is Afield

****

How Can A Person
Without A Cause
Be In Charge?

CHAPTER II

THE LOST, BLIND, AND FALSE EGO

THE   LOST   EGO

The Ego Entity must maintain a definite description of his True Ego, his Ego Task, his Ego Objectives and especially his Ego Goal, before him. Just like a person views himself in a mirror. And every time he looks at the Ego, etc., he should be able to clearly determine if he is where he should be in character development and with regards to his Ego Goal. Or see how far afield he has become.

Whenever the Ego Entity leaves the Ego Task, for whatever purpose that he uses to justify the deviation, he may unknowingly become the Lost Ego. A lost Ego can end up vigorously carrying out foriegn purposes and consequently begin developing into another type of Ego.

Thus, a Lost Ego is one because he doesn't recognize the fault in going away from his True Ego Task, and Goal, until he's so far afield that he can't find his way back to it. Like the lost sheep of the Bible or the Children of Israel in the wilderness. He fails to see the significance in staying involved with his True Task and purpose and without that before him he can't be seeing or is failing to follow his True Ego. Once he has been veiled he starts to veer.

An example of a Lost Ego venturing by blindness is a carpenter by trade who eagerly desires the job of an Executive Secretary, with no skills for the task. He must abandon his progression to become another type of Ego. This something he sees in this transition, this subtle allurement, is a status symbol. As a carpenter he was no longer being gratified or his level of self esteem had diminished. He no longer perceived rewards or attention for his work. The Ego Task had become redundant to him. He lost patience in waiting to reach his Ego Objective of becoming an Independent Contractor. He was an unsatisfied carpenter.

As an Executive Secretary, he may not know how to type 40 wpm. His filing skills may be off. No phone manners and he could care less if he's unqualified. However, he takes the position of an Intern Secretary because a friend said he'd get him a job and that in a year the Executive Secretary would be getting another position. Plus, he was blindly pursuing the status of position. The only true value in this transition would be to cure boredom and a lack of attention.

THE BLIND EGO

The Lost Ego then becomes the Blind Ego who may, if he doesn't check himself, ultimately create a False Ego. This Blind Ego doesn't see the true value in his own Ego Task, and may have never seen it. To be anything that you should be should, alone, cause self esteem of the highest. It should be rewarding within itself to accomplish your already laid out objectives. No task is guaranteed to be 100% mellifluous. Nor are you supposed to go for just the meretricious appeal and appearances of another man's task. You must see the real value of the task you have. The Blind Ego can't see it.

The Blind Ego, also, can't see that he is out of place in another man's shoes. He is seeing strokes, appealing words, welcoming gestures, tokens that give him a sense of pride. When the pride he should receive is in the hard earned accomplishments of the Ego Task. Besides that, everything just isn't for everybody. We are unique creatures and we need to know what's ours, how to reach it, and understand its true worth. We need to know ourselves and how to keep up with ourselves. And, we need to appreciate what we have and our lot in life. Its value can not be matched by what any other man can accomplish. Nor should we try to keep up with the Jones. Our objectives must be reached.

THE FALSE EGO

The Lost Ego who is the Blind Ego may eventually become the False Ego. He then develops an entirely different personality to match the needs of the new role and task. His pay may be cheaper, his craft stale, his real friends and family (which are all born a part of the True Ego) are falling away because of the image that they're not supposed to support. They become distant and isolated or they may begin to go places, venturing for compatibility.

The False Ego is basically someone else. He does what the job indicates. He may stop smoking because he's in a public place working. He may wear colors he doesn't like because certain colors are worn or allowed on the staff. His sense of humor may be toned down until it's stationary, because the Manager demands quietness and no joking around.

Now, if this False Ego continues he can lose his wife and friends. It is, therefore, imperative that people maintain focus on their True Ego and not allow their tempting attractions to other things, emotions, and positions, to lure them away from a reality that they have found to be their True Ego and its Goal.

The problem with a lost, blind and ultimately a False Ego is that everyone who knows the True Ego Entity relies on it for something (if they are a part of the Ego Circle) or he wouldn't have relationships or a family, etc. And his character, purpose, etc. is all like a magnet which draws people to it to form the Ego Circle. Once he alters his Ego, like was previously mentioned, the chemistry loosens the magnetic pull. People begin to fall off and pick up an entirely new set of acquaintances. The Ego Entity does likewise. The commonality has died.

Concerned wives, children, and friends may sometimes observe when people close to them may start going in alien directions. (they switch up on you is what some people call it) It is at this juncture that they need to inquire into what activity has drawn them away. Find out what's new? And most importantly, why? Why did the Ego change? Answers to these questions may help you save your marriage, keep a valued friend, keep a real good employee, and the like.

Failure to seize the opportunity of inquiry can cause a magnificent family to be destroyed. A good club leader can lose a hundred trusted followers, etc. Ego-ology would have people maintain close observation not only of their own True Ego, but of those dearest and closest to them as well.

Now, slight alterations of behavior may mean no more than the Ego trying new ways to reach the same goal. It can mean experimentation or adaptation. Sometimes a person may terminate a way of thinking and behaving and it turns out to be for the better. Also, some people may have been living in a False Ego all along. We simply need to be certain about it all.

To notice deviations from the norm is just the start of addressing a possible unwanted predicament. However, as long as you know that norm you at least know where the Ego has turned, even if it's yourself.

You must be tactful in approaching what you see as a peremptory decision of the Ego. If the Ego is lost you must find ways to cue it back. You can use attractive conversations, go back down memory lane. Or reminisce on things the Ego liked before about the Ego task and his goal in general. Get feedback. If he's apathetic about the subject, go to something else and then lead back into his Ego activity. Feel your way, and pay close attention

Another suggestion is to ask the Ego Entity if he would like for you to continue or terminate an activity he has given you that supports him and his task. Take him to commitments made in the past. Use others in his Ego Circle to do likewise.

There are other reasons why an Ego Entity may discontinue a task. J. Stacey Adams made one discovery noted in, "Inequity In Social Exchange," In Advances In Experimental Social Psychology, ed. L Berkovitz (New York: Academic Press, 1965), 176-299:

" Adam's version of Equity Theory. Central to the theory is the role of perception in motivation and the fact that individuals make comparisons.

It states that individuals form a ratio with the value of the input/outcome ratio with the thought of other individuals in a similar class of jobs. If the value of their ratio equals the value of another's they perceive the situation as equitable, no tension exists. However, if they perceive their input/outcome ratio as inequitable relative to others, this creates tension and motivates them to eliminate or reduce it. The strength of their motivation is proportional to the magnitude of the perceived inequity."

I would like to generalize this theory to include the comparison that one employee may make in one field with the rewards received by another in another field of work and say that an entity may feel cheated in life or in ratio to the position or status, even wages of another person and tension may result. An example is a correctional officer who feels that his job in a prison is far more dangerous than an officer working in a precinct. Even the pay is different. To generalize the theory even further, picture an officer on the beat who chases hustler's in the street every day. While he's living in a shabby apartment and driving an old Ford, they're living in a Penthouse and driving a new Benz. The tension of Adams theory is only one point. It's what the tension may drive the Ego Entity to do about it is the point that must be looked at and watched out for.

Say, for instance, the beat cop gets so jealous of the hustler he begins to envy him and starts hustling himself. Now he wants his piece of the pie, his day over the hustler, his fair outcome for being an officer..

Here are two other theories that can cause the Ego Entity to abandon his Ego Task and possibly make him feel inferior; according to Leon Festinger's Cognitive Dissonance Theory (1957) Tension results whenever people discover inconsistencies between their attitudes and their behaviors. This tension drives people to make attitudinal changes that will restore harmony and/or consistency. And Daryl Ben's (1772) Self Perception Theory, according to this theory people infer their behavior from watching their own behavior.

From these two theories, as can be applied to Ego-ology, we see that the Ego Entity can find himself second guessing his own Ego. However, he could gear or re-route himself back to his Ego from recognizing a deviation. Or he can see himself in relations to others and feel incompetent as he observes his behavior tension can result. This could all be a subliminal transference.

For instance, say you are told that the attire you must wear as a secretary becomes you, makes you look and feel like a million bucks. You go for it and begin to see it plus you begin to see how good you'll look once you get the Executive Director's position. Then you go home, put on your old jeans and head for a garage workshop. "This isn't me, " you proclaim. "I can do better with this new job." This isn't his True Ego. He is blind and has created a False Ego which changes his attitude and forces a change in his behavior.

But, what about the Ego Entity who just lags, when it comes to his Ego Task or pursuit of his objective? Can the lack of motivation be a form of blindness? Barbara Sher and Barbara Smith in their book " I Could Do Anything " states on page (64):

" When you see someone who won't try to go after what they want, they don't have safety in their bones. They sense some kind of danger with no apparent present cause, it's a good idea to go looking in the past." And at page (75):

" sometimes the only thing we do to avoid success is to refuse to be energetic on our own behalf. I'm not talking about anything extreme, just normal healthy eagerness, the kind every child starts out with. You started out with that energy too. Where did you lose it? Were you always this way? Or were you fearless and feisty until ten, or fifteen, or twenty five before you began to show confusion about what you wanted?"

The key to Ego-ology is to know that True Ego. And when that's not before you try to bring it back. If you are successful you may be able to restore or revive yourself or whomever it is who has gone astray and if you believe that your acquaintance is totally conscious of his/her actions and deem them appropriate to what his future may hold, then you may just have to adjust to the change. That could be the development of a new Ego. And may be even essential for the person's continued growth. Just check and double check before you concur or finalize your belief that this change is a must.

I must point out one other fact, a False Ego normally will become confused eventually. What he is and should be will not coincide with what he has become. It leads to self destructive attitudes, alcohol and drug addiction, maybe even suicide. There is where we find the injured Ego.

THE INJURED AND HEALED EGO

To Be Sick And Confused
Is To Be Unbalanced
So To Be Cured Is To
Even The Scales

****

To Be Drunk Means That
A Man's Sense of Judgment Is Off

****

Sometimes The Mind Does Sway
As The Pendulum
And Until The Push And Pull
Of LIfe Relaxes
We Will Still Have To Swing

****

Initiate A Thought In Life
Like A Prayer
That Will Always Bring You Back
To Wholeness
So That Sickness May Never Bare
A Permanent Hold Upon Your Being

****

To Be Sick Means
To Bare The Toil
To Carry The Affliction
But To Be Cured
Means To Make Anew

CHAPTER III

THE INJURED AND HEALED EGOS

INJURED EGOS

A Lost, Blind, or False Ego can lead to a confused, unbalanced, Injured or sick Ego. Where an Entity can develop inferiority complexes, anti-social behavior, and maybe even phobias, and even worse. For once a person becomes offended in life or from his role he normally retaliates, lashes out. Or he may repress such feelings, which may later erupt. In many cases a person may lose sight of repressed anger or frustration and it gets expressed in ways he may have never anticipated. Therefore, there's no way of stopping it or altering its course, or fulfilling its manifestation.

To be sure, an offended Ego can be the start of a great enemy. Even sometimes self hate can result, especially when the person finds no immediate outlet and begins to feel he is wrong either by what offended him or by not doing anything about it. And a confused Ego can choose wrong targets for different or wrong reasons. It can lead to psychopathic behavior and no role at all, but to isolate oneself. It can, also, cause domestic violence and child abuse.

Sick and confused Egos also may lead to misled Egos. Ones whose course or confused Ego task may lead a person to crime and deviant behavior or egotistical acts. Even Ego mania can be the result, along with many other mental conditions.

Characters like your modern day macho man, who feels that his weighty, aggressive, bogardish ways makes him more of a great man. And those with inferiority complexes who feel that their small size, lack of education, or physical handicap makes them incompetent, incomplete or inadequate are examples of False and confused Egos.

What really confuses the False Ego is that its image may have form for the Entity but it lacks in true substance. And once one has lived and portrayed all of this False Image's ways there is no real Ego fulfillment. There's still an emptiness, a void, a lack of true self esteem. Of course, the awareness of this lack is on the subconscious level. Even though on the conscious level the person puts on a front and goes through the motions. People pleasers.

He doesn't feel right. And, I guess you know how people become when they are not certain of themselves. One thing for sure they become afraid to be confronted on whatever it is they are not sure of.

Drug and alcohol abuse, and suicides are but a few escapes from the lack of self acceptance. This can easily become the behavior of the Lost, Blind, False and especially the confused Ego. And it leads to the Sick or Unbalanced Ego. The Ego seeks this escape or a replacement of reality because his current truth doesn't suffice his need for fulfillment of the Ego Entity and its task. For the True Ego and its Task is not being addressed. Or he feels too incompetent to aqccomplish his objectives, meet his needs or carry out his responsibilities.

In the case of many suicides people are reported as believing that the act is suitable to satisfy oneself by relieving oneself of life. (he assumes that the Ego Goal is complete and there's no more need for life). Some say that they are dying, also, so that they won't be a burden to others. (wouldn't it seem simpler to just adjust than to be a burden?) One man's burden can also be another man's pleasure. (it gives him something to help the former with)

Drugs and alcohol also work to release a person of a burden or responsibility. Or to make things lighter for the Ego. The Ego can then blame throw when things don't work out right. He proclaims, " I was high. " or "man, I was out of it." Then the behavior is supposed to be excused by others. Or this escapism works when an Ego just couldn't deal with certain mishaps, heartbreaks, disappointments, even simple nervousness or too much excitement causes an Ego to take to Drugs and alcohol. The latter is to regain balance or an equilibrium.

Man needs to be balanced in his Ego. Every aspect of the Ego Entity needs to be fed those thoughts that help it to grow in a positive way. To find this equilibrium one need only to break down his character and break down the requirement in reaching the Ego goal. As he reviews the ingredients to these he can find supportive ideas, people, motivators, events, etc. to gender recreation in activity as well as a reminder of needed behavior. Like, gymnastics for the Ego Goal.

Some lost realities as you may find in mental institutions are the result of an injured Ego. Some are as follows: "Schizophrenic" Entity. He has a separation between thought and emotion. He experiences delusions and bizarre behavior. There's the "Psychotic" Entity who suffers from personality disorders. He becomes disorganized and his contact with reality becomes impaired. Then you have the "Delirious" Entity who may suffer with fever, confused speech, hallucinations and can become uncontrollable and wild. And you have a "Demented" Entity who is mentally deranged. These are just a few conditions where the Ego is out of touch with his True Ego altogether and has no direct way to bring his own self back. Doctors seek cues to the Ego when these conditions have affected the Ego Entity to help bring them back.

Injured Egos are so because someone, event or experience has affected their way of thinking and believing. The Ego Entity can be thrown by the powers of others and influences that are more persuasive than the Ego Entity has been subject to or capable of controlling. Or he has not learned how to respond or react to a given stimuli or circumstance.

For instance, an illiterate Ego Entity whose intellect has not been developed enough yet and whose will consents to the logic of a more intelligent person; some like a mentor, leader, teacher, or role model, can be trusted to the point where the Ego Entity relies totally on this person. Then all of a sudden that person absconds or violates that trust between them. His dependency, then this sudden betrayal can easily make the Ego despondent, at an impasse in what choice of action to take and possibly detestable. He can feel tricked and that a lot was wasted. A climatic relationship, then the fall from it, can really damage a person's Ego.

Traumatic experiences such as a loved one's demise, a lovers rejection, a child's accident and the like can cause an Ego to choose, by being compelled, an activity that moves a person into a seemingly safe zone. Escapism is one such activity. This can easily happen with a religious person who feels that God is attacking his Ego.

Also sometimes a lack of knowledge can cause an entity to choose the wrong work or behavior as being appropriate. Simply because it is close to it and he has not yet made the Ego particular enough to make the distinction of the exact work.

Just look at a person who assumes a task from God to be his then he goes out and wars or kills all prostitutes because this is a sin and he is a death angel of the Lord. With proper knowledge of Biblical verse the person mentioned above would know that there is no current calling for death angels, especially those in men's bodies. Then he'd also only need to look at the events of prophecies. There has been no ascension. This mistake may be easy for some to make, who don't properly investigate alleged truths. Also because the Church is always speaking about these days being the last days. Then they point at certain events (in a rush to fulfill scripture) that appear similar and then claim it to be a manifestation of God's promise. Some people panic and some Ego Entities become confused about what course of action they must take in these times. They may ask, " Is there a need for the Ego task?"

Joseph J. Luciani, Phd. states in his book "Healing Your Habits"...what is left after your mind has become corrupted is a distortion, a pathetic shred of your true character...whenever intensity of emotion is locked in your head, psycho pressure is generated. Eventually this pressure causes your psychic thermostat to register too much emotional build-up. This causes the thermostat to click on, allowing a dissipation of pressure. ...whenever something is contained or confined within the psyche because of fear or the possibility of reprisal, it exerts pressure... The quest for perfection is fundamentally a quest for control, and a neurotic need for control is the parent of distrust.

Barbara Sher and Barbara Smith points out at page 179 of "I Could Do Anything":

" Imaginary obstacles are insurmountable, real ones aren't. But you can't tell the difference when you have no real information. Fear can create even more imaginary obstacles than ignorance can. That's why the smallest step away from speculation and into reality can be an absolutely amazing relief. "

Dr. Luciani points out in his book (pg. 48) that:

" Recent research shows that hospitalized patients who are rewarded by the attention of nurses or Doctors for moaning and whining actually report more discomfort and pain than patients who are only responded to whenever they stop complaining and show more self control.

...whenever you begin to stand up to whatever is doing the complaining or belly aching within you, you begin to cultivate an attitude that not only will put you in touch with your healthy, mature Ego but will also alter your experiences as well. "

And according to Carol Cox Smith in the book "Recovery At Work" the Ego states: pg. 34:

" Healthy functioning persons have lots of ways to cope. Their Ego-defense mechanisms are varied. Alcoholics have one Ego-defense mechanism, they drink. They drink when they're angry, sad, fearful, destitute, hopeless, morose. No matter what the problem, they drink. Healthy functioning people talk to a friend, jog, play tennis, scream into a pillow, go to a therapist, tap dance, go swimming, whatever is comfortable for them. At the same time, they are dealing with the problem in their own way."

The before mentioned Doctors and theories help to explain the mess we can get our Egos into and a little on what the problem seems to be. But there's more. Much, much, more.

Also, there are many hidden variables that can give us insight into the behavior of the Ego. Psychiatrists, psychologists, sociologists, criminologists, etc. are constantly diving into ideas and applying theories to solve the riddle of how to treat and cure the unbalanced Ego. They seek to determine what makes one condition one thing and another another. If they uncover another element they either say, "gee, we've got another condition, " or they'll say, " this is a new element in the condition we know of that we're just coming to realize.

Now, in Religion we have a catch all situation and statement. "Man has sinned," anything can happen from there. And you can call it anything you want from there. One thing for sure he did create that condition. Doctors want to know how?

There is a truth to the quest for knowledge if you believe that there are cures to the ailments we discover. What we find is discoverable by considering the problem as if it were two sides of a coin. We first must uncover what the known side of the coin is in order to determine the other side. Remember that the coin is made of the same substance, on both sides. The difference in the sides then is the difference in what's being portrayed. And for the problems of man's Ego you must continue to evaluate what the Ego is made of. What has been altered to create one condition? And what role does the Ego's belief play in all of this?

The SuperConscious holds the answers and even if it is willed to manifest it can not do so before its time. It's like seeking rain which can't manifest before the clouds appear. Nevertheless, in Ego-ology we would have you to continue your quest for self understanding and self development. The Ego and its cause must be studied. The truth must be measured. You must train your eye on the Ego's behavior.

HEALED EGOS

There are a lot of ways of addressing remedies for the ailing Ego, those who can't maintain focus on their True Ego or who have caused themselves to become unbalanced. However, as earlier stated, Ego-ology would maintain that the entity must be brought back to the acceptance of his True Ego.

There are some who have never reached the task of their True Ego, being lost from the start. Then come to find out later that they were wrong. Still they have planted and built an Ego system in the subconscious mind that can't just be ignored. When one seeks to change it there are built in defense mechanisms that are also learnt, which blocks the system from changing.

Of course, we know that some parents can become very dogmatic about what they think their child's Ego task should be. If they can egotistically choose their Ego task for them, they can also, by doing so, choose their Ego character and how it should develop. If the Ego Entity discovers that it would have been better to have pursued another work, which works out more natural for him, he's easily prepared or dexterous to perform, then he may determine to go for it.

However, let us diverge to consider some of the seeds of the early socialization process. Lets evaluate the power of words that give authority to the parent, which while rooted in the subconscious becomes a force to be reckoned with when attempting to change. Such phrases as "Honor Thy Father and Mother," "Respect Your Elders," and "Father Knows Best." These statements may challenge your belief in what you find to be your True Ego purpose since they may dissuade or be contradictory to your newly discovered self opinion.

Yet, as long as you are aware of these burly plants you can scientifically confront their influences and replant another attitude and belief in your mind to support what you have discovered about your Ego and its purpose.

In many instances, when an Ego Entity becomes confused about whether to honor some rule it has or choose another course it will retaliate, declare," I don't know what to do, " and then they might go out and get drunk or high. Which is just a form of Ego pacification that will still leave the Ego Entity unfulfilled.

The Ego Entity needs to make rational decisions on what to do about unwanating, conflicting, situations and be willing and eager to approach such problems with an open and sober mind and not by the dictates of Jack Daniels or Crack Cocaine.

To delay in addressing problems or in keeping up with one's own behavior, especially deviations from the Ego Entity's norm, may lead to an ailing Ego. And when one's rational solutions don't resolve, any longer, the difficulties one is facing it is time to check the Ego Entity's logic out or seek expert assistance.

There are too many problems and mental conditions that an ailing Ego can run into that intangles the Ego, and there's no need to always expect a lot of ready made answers. Each problem is unique and there are thousands of books on the problems of such Egos.

Nevertheless, Ego-ology reminds and encourages one to think about the being that should be and why it's not. It reviews the behavior that causes the Ego to go astray from its task. It, also, determines when the Ego is in its equilibrium, for that is when the Ego is balanced. That is normally when he is at his best. He can deal with problems better then too. Yoga and transcendental meditation are exercises that tend to help a person relax and find balance.

Positive thinking and having self confidence are essentials to any person struggling to become more and more of himself. And regardless of whatever pitfalls, stumbling blocks, or disappointments an Ego Entity might meet with if he approaches it right he can overcome it.

In one's thinking, capacity to comprehend, and level of literacy is the key to abnormality; it is also the key to sanity and normalcy. Curing means restoring, and science hasn't developed ways to cure the most extreme cases of abnormalities, especially those they classify as diseases and deformities. But the simpler problems of the Ego we can lick.

It is always sound advice to first consult your Ego Circle or those close enough to you to understand how you think when problems arise. Talk about the situations that bother you and get feedback. Make your conversattee pry and question your motives, emotions, or desires. And tape record the conversations to later see how you sound to yourself. Be expressive and not bashful.

Carol Cox Smith stated in "Recovery At Work" at page 35:

" friends help dispel fear. A network of friends can help you evaluate and change your lifestyle. If you are a loner reaching out to others for friendship it takes humility. Your pride tells you, I can handle it myself, but your new wisdom tells you, talk to someone. To whom should you talk to? Not to former friends if the friendships were based on shared addictions. Without addiction, there may be no basis for friendship. In fact, your recovery may seem a threat to or an indictment of, your friend's lifestyle. As soon as they know you are serious about staying clean and sober they may openly avoid you. If you go back to the same old haunts and try to maintain the same old friendships, you will feel uncomfortable, out of place, and you might start drinking or using again in order to fit in.

...to replace those feelings with happier, healthier ones, you need new friends who share your values and appreciate your goals and who can support you. You need new friends."

Ms Sher and Smith in " I Could Do Anything " states on page 224:

" Wounds of the spirit heal like wounds to the bone: in biological time. You can't tell a bone how fast to mend, you just let nature do its work. You can't hurry the process. All your broken bone needs from you is bedrest. The same is true of emotional wounds. All your hurt emotions need from you is to let the tears come , you're not going to jump right into optimism yet."

Whether the Ego has been offended, confused, or just plain dumb founded; or whether he has already sought to remedy his problems through drugs and alcohol, he has to reach and approach his real problem. Especially after he may have camouflaged his problems through various devices. And then employed various defense mechanisms to keep his true feelings curtailed.

The authors mentioned in this book have been active in addressing the problems of the Ego. They are quoted not as a mandatory element of treatment but as an optional tool, if you so desire or decide to use any of their suggestions or techniques. The same for any noted authorities.

Free Association is a Freudian technique that can be used to get in touch with the Ego's true problems or hang ups. You simply allow the mind to roam freely until it runs into his true wishes and wishes that he may really oppose yet he's seeking their manifestation. You can do this alone or with one or more members of your Ego Circle. You must be mindful, however, of the defense mechanism of rationalization, which will play off any thought or idea that doesn't sound appropriate or becoming of his newly developed or lost Ego.

Dr. Joseph J. Luciani, Phd. in his book "Healing Your Habits" speaks about a technique he uses called " Directed Imagination."

...Directed Imagination is a technique designed to realign your thinking, a good portion of which has been made unconscious by addictive habits. Whether you look inside and find the Beast, The Spoiled Child, or the Insecure Child, your work remains the same: to identify your regressive or destructive thinking and then clothe these thoughts with the appropriate characterization. Once dressed in these colorful mental images, the chaotic and confused thoughts of your addictive behavior will acquire a personality. At this point their destructive intentions will become exposed to the full light of the conscious Ego.

...what you have to do with any of the characters involved in Directed Imagination is to become an actor and act your script allowing yourself to become caught up in the illusion you create.

...The insatiable addictive desire of the monster within you is not you...you must separate yourself from that in you which has become so destructive.

You, your ego, should never become identified with this intrusive, alien, manipulator that has become a squatter in your life."

What Dr. Luciani is doing with Directed Imagination is to take your thoughts and give them a title based upon the kind of thought you have that competes against your real Ego and its success. Then you are to approach your competing thoughts until it submits to your true will and Ego. Of course, you can challenge any weak, hurt, or confused emotions.

However, if you try these techniques with your Ego Circle and too much hostility comes out and it leads to even greater problems in communication it may be wise to rest and return later to approaching that problem. And if you see the problems worsening you may need to consult professional help or join a Therapy Group with similar problems.

If your loved one or friend has suffered, or can't seem to adjust or realign himself to reality, he may need to be institutionalized. Our task as well as his/hers is to maintain focus on the True Ego. Remember that you are only trying to be a friend , not Sigmund Frued. Nor should you try to get your thing off on your friend. Be careful.

To be healed, to return to wholeness is the goal of the straying Ego. Again, one must first realize his true ailments. What belief has been affected? Why did the Ego choose to withdraw rather than confront the crisis? How and why did the Entity build his life to be whole only with a companion so that when the companion died or departed he declared that he couldn't or wouldn't go on? A companion or wife is an Ego help, not your Ego. It may be an alter Ego, but you're supposed to be self-sufficient.

Healing is a process, but it can also be like enlightenment. It can happen in a split second. In the twinkling of an eye.

Why is the question? The answer to why is the answer.

THE ALTER EGO AND SOCIAL EGO

A spouse is a female or male that lives
a natural life with another female or male
yet not legally married. Still they share
their lives as if they were

A spouse is also a person who has had
or caused the birth of a child
A wife/husband

****

Can we find a soul that is self same?
Can we engage in a unique affair,
Where we see ourselves again?

****

To be a part of a network
Full of untold concern
That's socializing

****

We meet our needs and combine
Our yearnings so well
One could be absent and
The task still done

****

Our alikeness has drawn us
To perform together
A symphony of chores
A lifetime of responsibilities

CHAPTER IV

THE ALTER EGO AND SOCIAL EGO

THE ALTER EGO

An Alter Ego is like another self. It can be defined as another aspect of oneself or another Ego of oneself, according to Ego-ology it is mainly more of a companion, partner, compatible mate or group. An Alter Ego is like a spiritual equivalent or a platonic acquaintance. It can also be a friend or spouse. It's like a reflection of yourself in others.

The members of a commune or group who share a common interest and have the same kind of Ego and task can be alter Egos. The likeness of oneself to the Alter Ego makes her/him easier to adjust to. It also compliments a person's behavior.

The Alter Ego supports one's reality and struggles to accomplish like objectives and Goals. They can easily be empathetic and sympathetic towards you and would know how to cater to your wants and needs because they are so self same.

An Alter Ego can be a Brother in a Brotherhood where, again, you adapt to the same norms and live by the same principles.

It is always wiser to find an Alter Ego to join in life instead of swallowing one's lust and heated compulsions. You can see people making unwise choices regarding mates quite often. A man will look at a big breast and a pretty face and leap right into an affair.

When the attraction is only physical or sexual, chances are that will be the only thing that has any genuine meaning. When there's no inter-change of ideas it's impossible to know what type of character you are approaching and proceeding to deal with.

It is far better to properly investigate the Ego to ascertain whether it's an Alter Ego or some other kind of Ego you are dating. Of course there are complimentary Egos that may support you and may never really know or understand you. People can choose you because of looks, status, or other superficial reasons. Which, in most cases, don't make for lasting relationships.

It's not hard to determine if the person you're with or have just met is an Alter Ego. You can quiz them or talk about your likes, ambitions, goals, etc. If you are a musician or just like music you may find an Alter Ego at a concert, opera house, a party, etc. You may be a connoisseur of art, therefore, you can venture to an art gallery or museum. Or, if you like sociology or Humanitarianism, you may find compatibility at lectures and seminars on subjects in the same area.

To find an Alter Ego is like finding yourself in others. That should always be easy to work with. And, too, you are an Alter Ego to that person. Therefore, they can see an easier affair with you. At least, if the compatibility is that close you know what to do for each other and about each other's situations.

Of course, there's a truth that says "man's greatest enemy is himself." So if you remember that principle you can also turn that to your benefit. Man becomes his worst enemy when his mind becomes self destructive. When there are aspects of himself that he feels makes him incompetant he may retaliate against himself in self hate. Sometimes handicaps get caught up in this kind of thinking. Sometimes when women and men are rejected for not being able to accomplish certain things or feats they convert to this way of thinking.

It is quite obvious that an Alter Ego can or may be able to be the first one to observe any such behavior or thinking that would indicate self hate, self pity, self destruction, self doubt and the like. But, what happens if the Alter Ego becomes jealous of the other person? He then can be your/his worst enemy. Again, if you are able to perceive these regiments of scourge you can prepare yourself to defend against their onslaughts.

Though the word Alter Ego normally implies a mate, we're using the more broader meaning when we view the term as a group. An example would be members of the same religion. These kinds of Alter Egos are unique to each other because they believe in the same religious doctrine, they are pursuing the same goals, they face the same challenges and they believe in the same God.

Since that form of Alter Ego knows so much about one another by virtue of the fact that they are subject to deal with the same circumstances they are in a position to assist each other.

Other groups where you might find Alter Egos are like the Old Town Jay Cees, 4-H Clubs, college fraternities, and even students of the same curriculum. They can be seen as self same because they have all chosen the same line of work. They may have developed the same kind of Ego which will become or cause their commonality.

Your Alter Ego may never be totally like you but enough for you to share a common bond. And, if you group up in an order or group, as such, when newcomers join, you have a son of the order, an initiate you can know as an Alter Ego and begin to help develop his Ego there. You will, more than likely, be familiar with most or all of the situations he's subject to be confronted with.

Jesus Christ once stated that his mother, sisters and brothers were they that did the will of his Father, which is in Heaven. (Matthew 12:50) because they had the same Ego and Ego goal in life, as the Father gave them spirit to have, they were automatically alike. They represent his Ego Circle.

An Alter Ego can also be your own son. Sometimes through hereditation various relatives will hold certain traditions and folkways. Some relatives will appear a lot like each other. And when they see these similarities it encourages them to become close.

Ego-ology would suggest that you take advantage of knowing and being near to your Alter Egos. Whether they be your mate, children, relatives, friends, groups or organizations. With them you are subject to share a most intimate and rewarding relationship. One that should be of full understanding and truth. For you will know far too much about each other to hide anything, and too much not to be comprehensive.

Pg. 54 (I And Thou- Martin Buber)

" These two attitudes, the I-Thou and the I-It. are essential to our nature. " The primary word - I-Thou can only be spoken with the whole being. The primary word I-It can never be spoken with the whole being.

We are born as individuals who are different from one another. We become genuine selves only as we respond to and enter into intimate relations with others. Through the Thou a man becomes an I."

THE SOCIAL EGO

The Social Ego is the Ego Image that is developed and manifested to become an adequate social being. I say "adequate" because if the Ego is inadequate chances are it won't be socializing for long.

The Social Ego must adapt to various personalities, circumstances, and environments in a very unique way, in order to get along and have meaningful communication with others.

Social interaction involves give and take; respect, compromises, and true consideration of the person(s) in the social setting, are essential components to the act of socializing

Therefore the Social Ego has to learn about the partner or group he intends to interact with. Their expectations, general attitude about things common to the group, how they comport with regards to newcomers in their lives, etc.,must be sought. The Social Ego must learn to adjust to what he learns.

However, this type of Ego adjustment may not have anything to do with the Ego task. He may be involved simply by virtue of the fact that his wife wishes to go out and likes to dance. That will get him into situations. Or your neighbors may simply want to be hospitable from time to time, inviting you over for dinner.

Since communication is the key to social interaction, the Social Ego must learn the dialect of his counterparts. This includes their jargons, habits, cultures, beliefs, norms, gestures, symbolism and the like. If the social counterpart requires compatibility in attire, exchange of gifts and other expenses the Social Ego has another burden he must overcome.

It is sometimes very conflicting for the Social Ego to maintain some relationships because of already established principles of the Ego Entity. Sometimes, religious, political and even sexual beliefs can create problems for interaction.

There are other problems that the Social Ego can run into in his attempt to be sociable, which involves his Ego task or his goal. For example, known celebrities can't go to certain places. Dating can be burdensome or tiresome and may exhaust their energy needed for a performance. They have to spend more money to be more private.

Sometimes your counterparts' mannerism, vulgarity and arrogance may conflict with how you wished she/he would treat others in an interaction, or simply people they come in contact with like waitresses, cab drivers, cashiers, etc.

There are also peer pressures that may create far too many demands on the Ego Entity. The whole point is not to allow social interaction or the Social Ego to cause an unbalancement or conflict with or deviation from the True Ego and its goal.

In Ego-ology the Ego Entity is admonished to remember himself while he attempts to get along with others not really a part of the Ego Circle. Since the Ego Circle involves persons that support the reality of the Ego and The Ego Task, he can be himself there, so to speak. When he's with others, however, he may have to bend a little.

The Ego Entity or Social Ego, in many cases, is likely to experience offensive behavior in social settings not of the Ego Circle or his Social Circle. And it can bring out the worst in him. He can sometimes experience feelings of inadequacy and hopelessness when he can't keep up with the demands or expectations of the group. He can, also, feel rejected and isolated at times for the same or other reasons.

When the Social Ego is challenged to comply with pressures of his group or any other setting it can have him living up to the expectations of others and consequently, lead him away from his True Ego. He can become a pretender or adapt to a whole new way of thinking.

On the other hand, he can retaliate, become assertive of his own opinions, and even become assiduous about his own Egos views; instead of assimilating the dominant beliefs of his peers.

Ego-ology would have the Social Egos acquaintances (his wife, friends, etc.) to confront his willingness to conform to ways too distant from his True Ego. (If he would not decide to do it himself) They may even suggest a change of activity to avoid the allurement.

Of course, as was suggested earlier, the Social Ego's spouse or friend can entice or encourage activity in line with the True Ego, even the selecting of different social settings altogether.

When it comes to joining different kinds of support groups, self help organizations, clubs, fraternities and the like, the task of leaving the group can be very devastating. Especially if you have become vulnerable by holding leadership positions or have become a respected spokesman. You have made commitments and followers have become dependent upon you. Those followers can become desultory and detach themselves from the group, if you leave.

That's what happens when people are compelled to participate in a program because of your diligence and performance. Therefore, once the Social Ego declares his departure and runs from the social interaction those who thrived off of that person's input or social Ego may stray or even leave.

It is imperative, therefore, to make sure that the group you join you can afford to stick with, in all its adversities. That's reflecting more social awareness and making sure you maintain social responsibilities.

If people are honest they can peep what kind of group they have joined long before they start making binding commitments. Even though the statement, " you can't judge a book by its cover," is true with regards to groups and organizations you can still decipher, by observation, what you've gotten yourself into.

Membership meetings, project meetings, and events sponsored by the Social Entity (the group) can give you vital insight in determining the true nature of the subjects in the group. That doesn't mean that the group has to be perfect. You just need to be realistic as to how much you can tolerate with others before you get too socially involved.

Some groups are shams; and even in those that are not some people within groups just may thrive off of creating problems. There are, also, others who get so far caught up in organizational politics that they just end up stepping on everybody's toes. They use gossip, blame throwing, and other egotistical devices to gain followers and demand their way. They even go at over throwing Board members or Chairmen to gain a tactical advantage.

Being the Alter Ego or the Social Ego and seeking the same is only seeking yourself in others. How to get along with yourself, then , is something you can learn. So, don't be afraid or cheap about your interaction.

It is best to approach both mating and socializing being aware that you are desirous of confronting your own behavior. And if you do so with an open mind it will be a very rewarding experience. Especially, if both of you seek to discover the same thing. Your True Ego.

THE POLITICAL AND RELIGIOUS EGO

" IN   GOD WE TRUST "

Without Principles There Are No
Measurements of Right And Wrong

****

Religion Is Established On Principles
Principle Is Founded On A God Will
A God Will, Thus, Creates A Law

****

The First Principle Man Violated
Of God's Is His Request of Man
To Be Obedient To His Request

****

Selling Out To Buy In Sometimes
Is What We Have To Do in life

****

To Be Political Is Not Always
An Easy Task When To Be
Religious Must Come First

****

It Is All Right that Every Right
Has An Issue, But Not So Good
When Every Issue Has A Right

CHAPTER V.

THE POLITICAL AND RELIGIOUS EGO

THE   POLITICAL   EGO

The Political Ego is a specific kind of Social Ego. With this type, the Ego Entity must adapt or maintain a certain stance or standard, as well as an attitude towards specific situations and topics of concern.

The Ego Entity that believes in a certain political or civic view can make that the basis of their interaction; as in joining a certain party such as socialist, communist, capitalist, etc. This doesn't have to be their only activity. It can be an extracurricular activity. Which means that this Egos True Ego could be something else.

However, the Political Ego that may be a part of an organization has a task within itself. For some, these Entities must adjust not only to people but changing views, advancing times, challenging opinions, etc. They are, basically, social leaders and/or concerned citizens interested in the affairs of the community, state and /or nation. They may also be solicitous about civil rights, religious freedom, etc.

A Political Ego, then, must be educated on those matters and be opinionated about how issues (of his political agenda) may affect those persons involved in his circle. Their motivation is seemingly altruistic. Some may, however, be power or status seekers.

Most Political Egos have moral standards that they pivot from and propagate. And, because of their beliefs they limit interaction to members of the party or those of similar beliefs.

Politicians that work for the Government (city Councilmen, Delegates, Senators, etc.) and lobbyists are two different Political Egos. The former works to appease and secure the lives of their constituents. While the latter strives to affect social changes for themselves and others of like mind and circumstances.

Political Egos find themselves at odds with other Political Egos all the time. They rally, boycott, fast, and fight to have their way. They even pray. Then there are other Political Egos who may simply belong to a particular civic organization, ethnic group, fraternity, veterans association, etc. Sometimes their plight is specific and sometimes it's general. Character wise they are more so humanistic.

Politicians are normally challenged more than other Political Egos. And that's because other Political Egos have their own opinions regarding the affairs in which they represent. Even if they don't force their views on others. Politicians, on the other hand, can have their views forced upon others because they are normally seeking and do establish laws and different modes of conduct through legislature.

Politicians can also be power and/or status seekers who may simply want to hold office and the salary that goes along with it.

When politicians must adapt to political pressures they may appear hypocritical, biased, prejudiced, etc. And people will constantly question their views and vie against them. Sometimes they might have to alter one view for another, sometimes just because they can't afford to maintain a particular view or course of action. His constituents may even compel and sometimes demand him to consent to contradictory ideologies. All of this can be misinterpreted.

But the other Political Ego, the advocate, may just keep his view in focus and build from that. He propagandizes to keep alive a certain belief. And changing times rarely changes this kind of Political Ego. Like the N.A.A.C.P, A.A.R.P., A.C.L.U., Gray Panthers, etc.

Of course, you have those parties such as Marxist, Capitalist, Communist, Darwinist, etc. they are not like environmentalists, economists, animal rights advocates, and other groups that simply politic. Yet, they all propagandize and propitiate to gain a tactical advantage. Thus their Political Ego is prepared to defend their positions and work towards accomplishing aims supportive of their objective.

In Ego-ology we want to, first of all, understand the basis of the Political quest that the Political Ego does have. Whether the Ego wants to be helpful or powerful. A Political Ego can become a very shrewd person or a very peacemaking entity. He can and may have to be recalcitrant and vituperate. But the motive is very important to ascertain. Does he wish to contribute to the development of righteousness or high morals or justice? Or is he prejudiced and wants a favored group in power?

Also, just because you are a Political Ego and someone else is doesn't mean you'll get along or be an alter Ego, unless you are in the same organization and subject to the same orientation you may not get along at all. A Political Ego can turn out to be your worst nightmare.

Even the Political Ego must determine his own true motive for being Political. Some people just have a way with people. Some are very believable. Some are good spokesmen. Some are very assertive and manipulative. He may have been better as a lawyer than a politician. Even though a lot of politicians are lawyers. A Political Ego needs to describe his genuine purpose for taking up the work.

And, again one must remember to be very careful about selecting Political Egos in your Ego Circle. Some, like those of special interest groups, may be less under pressure and may be self-same to the average Political Ego. However, they can be very dissimilar too. You need to probe to determine the type of Political Ego you are dealing with before you become too involved. Sometimes he may turn out to be very crude and ornery.

The problem of the Political Ego is that it is common to find him in situations that cause him to be very splenetic and tempestuous and these emotions can easily find their way back home with the family members or in a circle of friends.

Ego-ology would have you rightly prepared to deal with any unwanted attitudes from the Political Ego before it gets next to you or your kids. Pay close attention to him when he returns from any activity. (meetings, rallies, conventions, etc.) Try to read the Ego and then seek the proper response to the situation you see. Even if, prior to his arrival, you were upset about something, put your emotions to the side. See what he might need before you both end up in an uproar. Find things that relax his mind or change the clime, if necessary.

Be inquisitive and find out, off the bat, how the affair went. If he tries to be evasive chances are things were either average or bad.

Whether you're a Political Ego yourself or not, if your spouse or acquaintance is one it would be good to familiarize yourself with the political topics that interest the Political Ego he has. Make conversation with them and keep up on the subjects. He can use your input to sharpen his wits.

You, also, need to know when he needs to rest or go on a vacation. Or when he needs to address other pertinent matters of concern that may affect your family, you, or your relationship with him. Make note of all pressing times and show your confidence in him and his plight.

THE RELIGIOUS EGO

The Religious Ego is an Ego that has adapted a religious belief as an Image for his Ego. His character is a reflection of the dictates of his religious doctrine or belief. He takes upon himself the nature of a Divine Entity, if it's a Holy religion. Or a Devilish nature if it's an unholy religion. (since a Devilish religion is surnamed the occult or dark sciences. We won't hold that subject as a topic in this book. Since it's supposed to be a secret we'll leave it there)

The Religious Ego normally follows the examples set by the prophets, gurus, sages, and Holy priests of his order or faith. As in Holy religions he attempts to fashion himself (His Ego and lifestyle) just as it is written to.

Prophet Mohammad, Jesus Christ, Hare Krishner, Buddha, Moses, and the like are revealators and spiritual guides who are supposed to have taken a spiritual journey on the paths of their orders and they reached certain blessed heights. So initiates or new comers begin on the same path.

The Religious Ego is also one who lives a ritualistic life. Rituals help a person adjust psychologically to a following or repetitious act. Like not eating swine, abstaining from eating meat, meditation at certain times of the day, prayers periodically, etc. In the religious context it's like Holy communion and making salat. These rituals have meaning as a tool for atonement, attunement and in some cases simply decent habits or reminders. These acts also help to establish the Religious Ego.

The Religious Ego and Ego Entity can conflict, these two must find a way to merge into one. In religious practices man is taught to deny the Ego Entity in order to accept the Spiritual Ego. The Spiritual Ego is a part and Image of God. Therefore, the Ego Entity has to be transformed by the renewing of his mind or Ego. Man then is known first as the Ego Entity fashioned by the world. He is subject to the laws of the Ego Entity and its environment from birth and as he has developed.

Thus, in the religious context the Ego Entity is a Blind, Lost, and False Ego. And even a Sick Ego needing spiritual healing. He is this because he is not in harmony with God. He doesn't know or do his will.

Most Spiritual Egos who become such at a later stage in life have to combat the Ego that has been developed, with all of its vices. This becomes a constant struggle which requires submission to the practices and principles in religion.

The Ego Entity and the Spiritual Entity can, on the other hand, compliment each other. Say for instance, the Ego task is to sing. A professional singer turned christian becomes a gospel vocalist or choir member.

In all cases, the Spiritual Ego is admonished to separate himself from anyone or thing that may hinder his willingness to submit to the Spiritual doctrine or faith. The Religious Ego who is just becoming such must live a dual natured life, like a Multiple Ego. He may be one way in his ordinary life and almost completely different in his religious life until he can live an entirely religious life.

This dual life can pose a drastic problem if the Ego Entity is well established in what his Ego work is. He can lose loved ones, friends, and sometimes partners, after deciding to be a religious person. This happens because he is changing and the Ego Circle will not see the same person they became one with him for. Their purpose together would be diminishing. Like was discussed earlier, the chemistry changes and the commonality dies when the Ego Entity decides to leave his Ego task or chooses another one.

Most religious doctrines will actually request that the Spiritual Ego lose or abstain from old acquaintances and choose new ones of that faith he has chosen. You may have to because the Ego Circle won't have the same person to deal with and the compatible traits may shortly vanish. Subjects of conversation may become totally obsolete because the Religious Ego can no longer identify with or partake of certain habits, manners, behavior, and other former activity.

For the person who's already married, Ego-ology would advise the wife or husband to be considerate of the wishes of your spouse. Their religious aspirations may be better. Apparently, the Religious Ego thinks that it will help him. Therefore, it's worth checking out, for their sake at least.

You may also need to familiarize yourself with his religion, in order to know what to expect and do for your spouse or friend. If the religion requires a special diet, like 7th Day Adventist members who don't eat meat, or Muslims who don't eat pork, then you must prepare his meals to accommodate the need to substitute or change his eating habits.

Their need for privacy and a prayer life must be acknowledged. When they are reading a Holy doctrine they may not want to be interfered with. It's best to suggest and establish certain times for Holy reading and prayer. So that you will know the exact time he wants to be alone with his God. Plus, noise must be to a minimum and music may not be preferred or allowed at all, at least around him.

The Religious Ego won't be a sinister person, ordinarily, so you can rest your nerves on that point of concern, unless he's a Devil worshiper. It's best to watch out for weird, peculiar, behavior. Especially anything that might indicate demonic rituals. Those kinds may even believe that they are supposed to offer up blood sacrifices. And some of those are completely nuts. So, if you do observe strange behavior you need to make an inquiry into his practice.

Both the Political Ego and Spiritual Ego must maintain certain standards of living lest they become hypocritical. (a mockery and a farce) The Political Ego may come into conflict and hardships because he is faced with altercations, wins and losses. But the Spiritual Ego may come into hardships and conflicts through bouts with the devil and the sufferings associated with change. In addition, they become very sensitive to the plight of other Spiritual Egos close to them.

You as a spouse or friend must play the role of a comforter, and a listening ear. Your patience will always be in demand and your tolerance must remain at the forefront at all times.

MULTIPLE EGOS

What Can Be The SameThing?
Even The Passing Of Time
Makes Us Something Different

****

We Become One Way For Love
Another For Hate

****

As A Social Being I Become
Like You. But Alone
I Can See The Sun

****

Just Because A Man And
Woman
Become Adults
Doesn't Make Them Parents

****

Though We Portray Many
Images
Flowing From One Inner
Being
We Must Remember The Essential
Center
That Makes Them All
One

CHAPTER VI.

MULTIPLE EGOS

Multiple Egos are a manifestation of the development of more than one Ego. This stems from the Ego choosing more than one Ego Task which are different in form and/or substance from each other and requires different traits from the mind of the Ego Entity.

For example, the Multiple Egos can be a Musician/waiter, Doctor/Politician, and Minister/Soldier. As a Musician he remains a distance from his audience and he is exalted. He is looked up to and has great appeal. Yet, as a waiter the same person is debased. His demeanor is unappealing and he is a servant. As a Doctor he has a Code of Ethics that he must adhere to and make it the foundation of his behavior in his medical profession. Yet, as a Politician he must maintain the stance of his constituents in matters that are totally contradictory to the ethics he must proclaim in his medical practice. And, the Minister who preaches that " Thou Shalt Not Kill." Yet, as a soldier he must take up arms and kill to protect, defend, or simply appease a demand made by the Government.

I chose conflicting Multiple Egos, first, because in order to accomplish them the Ego Entity must reject one behavior and rationale to adapt another one. These were totally opposite and the Ego Entity must die of one ideology to live in the other and vice-versa.

What makes it a different Ego is the norms of the Ego. This term is not to be confused with the psychological condition called Multiple Personality. In this medical condition an Ego Entity actually becomes another person with a distinctly different personality, another name, another voice for each character, another style of , etc. (Sybil) Some may want to call this phenomenon an extreme form of Multiple Egos. However, since Multiple Personalities is a sickness I won't venture to adapt the condition as the same as Multiple Egos, which is normal.

Multiple Egos can also be interpreted as Multiple Roles. However, a role is more of a portrayal than a real thing. And it has a short duration, ordinarily. Here in Multiple Egos you must become a particular kind of person for a specific reason.

Look at a student who goes back to his neighborhood intellectualizing. He is quickly classified as a nerd. To overcome this he must change or allow another Ego to develop. Instead of saying, "Good Evening, How are you doing?" He may say, " Say, Flavor, what's happening?" Just to say the latter from the former requires a change in character. Try it!

Whatever circle you find yourself in has its own norms and if you have varying groups you belong to you must have different characteristics in them. Those characteristics define an Ego. Even though the original Ego isn't necessarily lost in the interchange, you have another Ego according to the situation and circumstances. That is another degree of Multiple Egos though it isn't as extreme as having contradictory personalities.

Sometimes an Egos development may cause one Ego to abandon the other Ego simply because of an extreme difference in behavior. Thus, he establishes a priority. Like the Minister who's also a Politician and has to decide in favor of subjects such as abortions, mercy killing, the death penalty, etc. If his constituents request his representation for something immoral he's supposed to represent their views unwaveringly and diligently. However, he may decide to abandon the Political Ego for the Religious Ego altogether. Then he'd have to decline from the task. And, of course, he wouldn't make for a good politician either. Unless he represented religious views only.

Ego-ology would suggest that a person pay attention to what he is getting himself into when he decides to develop some form of vocation or engage in some activity that isn't compatible with his already established Ego. Don't just follow flimsy curiosities. Be careful. Be wise before you find yourself living a contradictory or hypocritical life.

Again Ego-ology would have you observe your spouse or friend and especially children when they begin to choose behavior or a line of reasoning and then start switching up. Make sure your loved ones know the pros and cons of any pertinent decisions they have to make with regards to a change of role. Compare the expectations in the new role to that of the old roll. Especially with growing children because deciding what to do in life and then changing after you've started working towards one goal can amount to a waste of time, energy, and resources.

This constructive criticism of altering Egos isn't intended to deter positive intention or a well considered change of heart. Being versatile is not a crime and can prove to be very necessary. The problem can come in when the role requires a total conflict of roles and the Multiple Egos then experiences a conflict of interest or he (the Ego Entity) can become confused when he has to decide on the role to be chosen.

A split personality and a person with Multiple Egos can appear to be the same. (that's when the layman uses the term to mean a person keeps switching up on someone). However, some people can choose several Egos to become and never have any problems with it. The key to the concept is not to just role play. You must become a perfect replication of the entity you must be, like an actor. Actors become so engrossed in being the person to be portrayed that they, practically, become that person; their walk, talk, accent, style, emotions, way of thinking, etc. The by-polar condition is similar so is homosexuality/ lesbianism where the person seems to be one way on the masculine side but when the feminine side comes forth they change. They may even switch up how they will deal with a situation because they are now their female. Or the male/female who thinks it's time to be gangstafied.

For an average Entity, however, the idea of becoming only means that if you take on a task you must become it to the best of your ability. To be a Police Officer doesn't mean to be a crook. To be an adult doesn't make you a parent. Thus, when you take upon yourself the role you take up the responsibilities that go with it. At times and to varying degrees you will have to not see certain aspects of yourself to live and perform the task of another development of yourself.

Barbara Smith and Barbara Sher make a statement and ask a few questions to those persons seeking to establish another Ego in "I Could Do Anything." pg. (222 to 223):

" For you to start again you'd need to be a different person with a different goal. Not all former singers want to teach music. Not all former athletes want to coach. That's not you. You loved exactly what you had." at page (105):

" If you were ten people, what would each of you do with your life?" at page (106):

" Which life can you devote yourself to this coming year? Which life can you do when the first one is completed? Which activities can you do for 20 minutes or less each day? Which ones can you do on a weekend? Which ones can you do once in a while?"

Flexible personalities are everywhere now-a-days and it takes a very wise person to be able to keep up with a diverse person with Multiple Egos. Wives and friends may be called upon to help the Ego Entity to become each different Ego he must develop, regardless of how opposite these personalities or Egos may end up being. And since you will be faced with differing Egos you have to be very understanding of the problems each task holds. It will make you a social scientist in no time. But never be too quick in stigmatizing behavior as zapped out when it's only peculiar. Or mentallly insane when it's only a person's way of adjusting to different roles or dealing with the unknown. For the situation may only require adequate inquiry into its nature or cause. And, never make factual judgements of the unknown. For sometimes you can make a situation worse than it is just by believing that it's that bad.

And with Multiple Egos you must remember that in order to use the tool of empathy you must be able to put yourself in another person's shoes. Therefore, you have to be able to identify with each Ego development and you have to determine where one ends and the other begins.

It may look strange trying to keep up with a person with different Egos and Ego tasks. However, if that's what he must do or want to do, then that's what he must do.

Pg 484 (Living Issues in Philosophy-titus, Smith, Nolan)

" Closely allied to the concept of Brahman is the concept of the self, or soul or atman. The true self of each person is identical with Brahman. From the transcendental standpoint the self is immortal, free and one with Brahman. The divine nature of the self is veiled but not destroyed, by false images and ignorance. The true destiny of the self is the retaliation of this relationship with Brahman. From the phenomenal standpoint, there are many different selves enmeshed in the world of affairs and seeking deliverance from the round of births and death."

PART II.

EGO-DEVELOPMENT

****

                                        *

                                        *

                                        *

                                        *

                                        *

                                        *

                                        *

                                        *

                                        *

                                        *

EGO-OLOGY AND CHILD DEVELOPMENT

Conception To Inception, Then We
Perambulate
Things Unwanting We Obviate
Through Our Perilous Times
Let Us Not Become
Prevaricate
As We abnegate the Worst
Of Ourselves To
Become Our Best

****

Many Are The Experiences
Standing Before A Child
On His Path To Unfoldment,
Fulfillment, Elevation
May We Pass Unto Them The Gems
Of Our Gathering
We That Believe In Tomorrow

****

To Help One To Grow Means
To Tend To, To Nourish
To Cultivate, To Breed
Always Viewing With A Watchful
Eye
An Element Of The Future

****

CHAPTER VII

EGO-OLOGY AND CHILD DEVELOPMENT

Child development is a very complicated and delicate process that involves physical, mental, and spiritual challenges to growth. Parents have to assure the child's safety, education, and well being.

One of the most essential aspects of growth is the development of the Ego and assigning to it a purpose in life. It is difficult to say what a child will become but we do know that the key to it lies with that child. Parents sometimes attempt to mold a child (egotistically) after themselves, and many children will buck on their parents, early, if they perceive that their parents are dictating how their life should be. Even if the parent is accurate in giving advice, etc. Just because the child wants his own independence, he may shun advice. And take a beating for it.

Therefore, the parent should keep the child's wishes first and in clear view, when it comes to what they want to be, naturally. And encourage the child's own choosing in an Ego Goal.

Most kids may suggest several different goals to pursue as an Ego Goal or career choice. However, the parent must be able to see or perceive the True Ego. If a child says, "I want to be a singer when I grow up." then says, "I want to be a lawyer too." The parent may have to help determine if one is a hobby choice or one is a career choice. If singing is a hobby he may become both. However, if singing is the career choice a parent would have to really question why he wanted to be an attorney? Or he could be geared towards an entertainment attorney, if it wouldn't crowd his work as a performer.

Heredity sometimes can give you some indications as to what to consider for the child's Ego Goal. For instance, some families have all Doctors, or all politicians, or all ministers, etc,. as their Ego Task. Or they may all just fit in one family business that requires varying types of positions.

However, the truth about what the child should become still lies with the child and his decision about it.

By the time an Ego Entity reaches the High School level it's about time to finalize what the career might be. Especially if college is a must. High School students may have to work to save for tuition or at least help with the expenses. These early responsibilities can prove to be helpful as a learnt behavior to be utilized in later life. Also, if the child goes to college his classmates will represent an Ego Circle for him and may prove to be real good friends as they step into their career choice.

There is, however, no assurance that even the career choice is the Ego Goal. Sometimes people choose careers based upon the feasibility of getting a good salary for it. Say, for instance, there's a prediction indicating that social workers are coming in demand, by 2025. Therefore, there's a sure thing job if you get a B.A. in social work. A lot of Egos will develop into social workers, which may or may not be their True Ego's Goal.

Should they lose their True Egos Goal for the sake of the need for money, statue, or power? I should say not, for therein lies the purpose for one's existence. And if an Ego has to deviate out of blindness or because of a need for opportunities to support them, etc., they need to get back on the right track as soon as possible. It's like a child whose True Ego was to be an actor. However, as a child he ended up in the fast lane chasing pretty girls and slick fashions so he steps out of school, (drops out) starts selling drugs and ends up in prison. There he comes to the realization that he has left his True Ego and its goal. He, therefore, goes back to school, gets a G.E.D., takes up a relevant subject in college, (which may be directly or indirectly supportive of his realignment back with his Ego Quest), makes parole for good behavior, goes back out and takes up a course or two in acting and then starts seeking a job. Though he may have been delayed, he can now fulfill his life's goal.

Therefore, the parent must keep a watchful eye on the True Ego and its earliest pursuits. For the parents have to help him develop his Ego. That's more important than the job he may choose.

Look at how many models that have college degrees and in different fields of work who end up never using any of that knowledge.

So what do we look for in determining the Ego's wishes? Well, you need to ask the child as early as possible about his/her likes, dislikes, ambitions, goals, etc. Make a list of the answers and then see which ones the child goes for the most. Which gives him/her the most enjoyment? He/she shows dexterity in what areas? Which challenges does the child take to and accept the most?

While making your observations of the child you have to stay in the back- ground, so to speak. Not making decisions from him. You just buy the crayon, videos to watch, find shows (even educational ones) to turn on the T.V., etc. And after a while you ask the same questions to see which goals are being kept.

To stay ahead of the game, you can read up on the subjects that your child has chosen. So that you can have some input on when he's right, wrong, or lacking something essential for the tasks he has. For instance, if he wants to be a carpenter, get a few books on carpentry. Know different kinds of wood, nail sizes, types of structures for homes, etc. conversate with him on his subject. (don't try to outdo him too much) He may accept the challenge to stay ahead of you.

Ego-ology would keep you intune with your child's way of thinking. Also, his general attitude about basic normal things like the types of girls he likes and why? What kinds of recreation does he favor? What kinds of movies interest him most? Etc.?

As your child grows it would be wise to double check on those basic desires he had at first. See which ones were maintained. It can tell a lot about the Ego. It's always best though, to never make decisions for them, unless they just don't understand enough about the problem or circumstances. Then you may need to explain the situation and whatever options exist.

Using suggestions would be safer than appearing to be making decisions for the child. But keep up with the decisions that he makes, and give advice especially on factors detrimental to those issues.

Another good idea is to get close to his girl friends and friends in general. Ask them questions about him, unless it irritates him to have you signifying in his affairs. Sometimes if you start a conversation and kind of lead into certain subjects people will talk about them. That way you won't get accused of bringing subjects up to pry.

All of this is to keep up with the growing Ego. To help it you must simply feed to the best ideas and be cautious of the detrimental ones. Even though kids may resent your signifying (don't get caught too much) sometimes they will also resent you for not inquiring some. They'll feel that you don't care enough.

At this point we would like to look at a few of the possible pitfalls and conflicts the growing Ego may encounter if certain basic psychological needs aren't met. Some of these problems may lead to drug and alcohol abuse.

For starters we will look at Erik Erikson's eight stages of Human Development:

ERIKSON'S EIGHT STAGES

Stage and Approximate Age DESCRIPTION	Psychosocial crises	
Infancy (0-1)	Trust versus Mistrust	Infants learn to trust that their needs will be met by the world, especially by the mother, if not, mis-trust Develops.
Early Childhood (1-3)	Autonomy ver-sus shame and Doubt	Children learn to exercise the will to make choices, to control themselves; if not, they become uncertain and doubt that they can do things by themselves

Play Age (3-6)	Initiative versus guilt	Children learn to initiate activities and enjoy their accomplishments, acquiring direction and purpose; If they are not allowed initiative, they feel guilty for their attempts at independence.
School Age (6-12)	Industry versus Inferiority	Children develop a sense of industry and curiosity and are eager to learn; if not, they feel inferior and lose interest in the tasks before them.
Adolescence (12-20)	Identity versus Role confusion	Adolescents come to see themselves as unique and integrated persons with an ideology; if not, they become confused about what they want out of life.

Young Adulthood (20-30)	Intimacy versus Isolation	Young people become able to commit themselves to another person; if not, they develop a sense of isolation and feel they have no one in the world but themselves.
Adulthood (30-65)	Generativity versus Stagnation	Adults are willing to have and care for children to devote themselves to their work and the common good; If not, they become self centered and inactive.

Mature Adult (65+)	Ego Integrity versus despair	Older people enter a period of reflection, becoming assured that their lives have been meaningful, and they grow ready to face death with acceptance and dignity; if not, they despair for their unaccomplished goals, failures, and ill spent lives.

Erikson has portrayed the central psychological needs of the human entity from infancy to the Senior Ego or last stages of human development. At each developmental stage we can see that if the Ego isn't gratified there are noted repercussions. As you follow your own child's growth you can be mindful of each stage as he lives them. You may even be able to break those stages down into smaller groups. By all means, do your own observing.

Erikson points out that the play age is when the child begins to show initiative. This seems to be when the child starts to formulate an idea of purpose and establishes some direction. The school age is when he starts seeking his Ego Circle based upon his early quest of his Ego Goal. If he is denied the opportunity to be assertive, independent and with direction he becomes uncertain about his ability to achieve what he wants. He may also start to feel incompetent and inferior.

Another problem that can develop and interfere with the child's growth is when the child is over cared for. When they become spoiled or taken care of so much the child doesn't have the chance to learn for himself.

Dr. H. Paul Gabriel and Robert Wool in their book called " The Inner Child " notes five stages of growth for the child: (1) The Age of Dependency (birth to 14 months), (2) The Age of Exploration (14 to 30 months), (3) The Age of Communication (30 to 48 months), (4) The Age of Separation (48 to 60 months) and (5) The Age of Early Independence. (60 to 72 months) pages 4 to 5:

Stage 1: The Age of Dependency
(birth to 14 months)

This time is when your infant is almost totally dependent on you, unable because of his lack of motor skills and physical development to do much of anything by himself. For him it is a time of confinement, but during this period of seeming inactivity occur the first stages in the development of the child's personality.

Stage 2: The Age of Exploration
(14 months to 30 months)

The infant can finally move about on his own and begins to explore his universe. He starts testing his autonomy and hears an awful lot of " no, no, no" and "don't, don't don't" from his watchdog parents. Your baby will experiment with his new environment. He will put fingers into electric outlets, crawl into kitchen cabinets, pull on table cloths. It is also the time Freud labled "anal," and during this period you and your child will first come into substantial confrontation and conflict.

Stage 3: The Age of Communication
(30 to 48 months)

Your child's curiosity is tremendously heightened. He begins to test reality, to strike out in the world. He is developing skills of communication and is making up stories, fantasies, fears, monsters. Culture begins to make new demands with the start of nursery school. This is also a time of sexual awakening and curiosity: Freud's Phallic period and the beginning of the Oedipal period. It is also Piaget's concrete period, Erikson's period of initiative. It is a time of Narcissism and of Freud's pleasure principle.

Stage 4: The Age of Separation
(48 to 60 months)

Your child's struggle with growing up begins in earnest, his sexual curiosity increases, and Freud's Oedipal conflict is intense. It is a time of showing off, of saying "look at me." Your child will begin to do things by himself, and little girls will start dressing up, playing house. It is a period when your child trusts you but also resents you.

Stage 5: The Age of Early Independence
(60 to 72 months)

During this period, your child begins an intense struggle between becoming independent and fearing that independence. He now has enough motor coordination to master numerous tasks, to sit at a table, to draw letters. Cultural influences are strong and the matter of goals and competition with other children enters his and your lives.

On page 181 they also point out that the Age of Early Independence:

" As your child steps into society there are a number of new activities and opportunities for her. Try to keep them under control.

It's quite a range. You might want to start taking her to church or temple. There may be a story program at your local library that sounds good. The Y may have a ceramics class and you might have heard of a dancing teacher that's good with children. Test and choose."

Dr. Luciani also comments on another aspect of the self and a parents role with the developing Ego; "Healing Your Habits:"

"...your sense of security depends on whether your developing Ego had the opportunity to experience and feel embraced by a competent loving adult. Such an adult would have allowed you to be carefree and unconcerned with anything beyond your own natural development. When a child grows up in such an atmosphere, anxiety and insecurity are reduced, if not eliminated. If, on the other hand, you were brought up with inconsistency, conflict, or abuse, then insecurity probably flourished

...take for example, the parent who, out of "love" never stops taking care of the child, who is learning to handle life. He or she may learn only how to remain a child. This unique type of insecurity can leave an adult fearful of life's responsibilities. Such adults expect to be taken care of and become absolutely hysterical at the notion of being alone.

...all security begins with love. When love is inconsistent, overbearing, or absent, the child becomes more and more compulsive about finding security."

Be the first to know when the Ego is straying and attempt to catch it before it gets lost, blinded, false or sick. Watch your own behavior in raising and relating to your child, spouse or friend. And remember some of the suggestions in this book to regearing them back on the path of their True Goal.

When you're dealing with the developing Ego you must consider the whole early socialization process. What part does the school, family, peers and maybe religion play in the child's growth?

Ego-ology would have you pay close attention to the influences coming from each group that affects the Ego's growth. For in between them, confusion can be there. Especially, when the peers don't agree with what the family says he should be. And the family doesn't agree with what the school is saying he should be. Or the church may be in disagreement with all of them. It is then that you must be the unbiased coach. And keep negative grooming down.

I have come to believe that 90% of persons incarcerated have deviated from their True Ego and it's Goal by taking up criminal activity as a task. They normally begin to stray at a young age. Truancy, getting high, buying expensive clothes that they can't afford without crime, and being promiscuous.

Those are typical behaviors of most convicts. They live in the fast lane by living a fast life, cheating. Some end up lacking responsibility. Many of them have kids that they don't take care of or help to raise. They leave that burden on their baby's mother or the grandparents. Sometimes their parents will reject taking their responsibilities, so they duck asking them. On the other hand, some go to prison and find themselves, put themselves in check, and start rebuilding their lives. However, some never return to their True Ego. Don't let this happen to you and try to help your loved ones. Appeal to their reasoning mind.

Be attentive and involved with the growth and development of the Ego. Make it an Ego task of yours, for that's what it is for the parent and part of the description of a true friend. The entire Ego Circle functions the same way or what good would they be to the Ego.

EGO-OLOGY AND GENDER, CULTURE,
RACISM AND HEREDITATION

We do, throughout our lives,
Confront the dualistic thought
Produced by racism, our division,
When there's only One Family
The Human Family
One Race
The Human Race
****

Culture breds us
Yet, it does not carry back far enough
We would all have the same culture
I guess we began again
At the split

****

How often do we contradict ourselves
Must we claim that
Adam and Eve are but a myth?
Do we deny the parents' of existence?
Should we know them?
Should we know them?
****

Male & Female
We do carry our role
Yet, do we compromise? Yet, do we honor?
Yet, do we merge? Yet, do we transcend?
Yet, do we return to God who is neither?

CHAPTER VIII

EGO-OLOGY AND GENDER, CULTURE, RACISM, AND HEREDITATION

We shall now turn our attention to four other variables that serve to fashion or at least influence the development of the Ego. These four are gender, culture, racism, and herediation. Religion can be included. However, it can be seen in culture, racism and herediation.

We would fail to totally understand the Ego's behavior and way of thinking if we didn't consider these very vital factors in the early stages of an Ego's development. Those norms, mores and folkways that may lay dormant subliminally and may never emerge enough to be seen. It would, therefore, take our investigation to conclude the unknown.

It is a truth, on the subject of gender, that in most societies the male is required to be masculine and carry out such functions, and the female be feminine and carry out such functions as are prescribed or negotiated by the society or the persons of a household.

However, there are instances where the society or Circle or situation may require a different adaptation. Such is the case with one parent homes where a female is raising a male. You may notice quite often, in our modern day society, that many men carry out responsibilities at the home that were once only assigned to women, such as cooking, washing the dishes, changing diapers, doing the laundry, etc. These developments have led to the establishment of a masculine/feminine adjustment that sometimes must go backwards and forwards between partners. It can also create role conflict and may lead to role confusion.

Therefore, the male/female who must monitor or support a spouse who has to adjust his/her Ego to sex indifferences must pay close attention to the possibility of unbalancement, frustration, stress, etc. that can cause drastic changes in a persons attitude. Especially after that person has learned the common roles and expectations his Ego is supposed to have in its natural masculine or feminine establishment.

Sometimes a male who has to be supported by the female, who maintains a position of benefactor, breadwinner, etc. can suffer from a feeling of inferiority. He may also develop a habit of slashing out at his female counterpart to diminish her status. Or he may generalize this complex to include women in general, where he begins to attack or insult them. As if they're trying to be too high or besides themselves when they become the least bit assertive. And, of course, these attitudes can lead to role or self rejection.

The spouse who happens to observe a conflict because of her/his reversal of sex roles or versatillity in responsibility, to any degree, need to be inventive enough to approach the problem and move towards helping the spouse balance his fears or worries.

Cultural influences can also cause a great deal of problems, especially if you haven't studied the culture of your spouse or friend. Take for instance asian Americans. They are culturally non communicative of personal feelings, since emotional expressions are seen as a sign of immaturity. They are verbally non-aggressive and self deprecating. They believe that time is flexible so there is no need to hurry or be punctual except in extremely important cases. Family members are also expected to submerge their own behaviors and feelings in order to further the welfare of the Family and its reputation. These characteristics come from Elizabeth Randall-David, Ph.d, in "Strategies For Working With Culturally Diverse Communities and clients."

She claims the following characteristics of Hispanics/latinos: males are free to have extramarital affairs, females are not. Having women is necessary to identify as male. More concerned with the present than the future. Polychronic time orientation - engaged in several things at the same time.

American men and women, if they are not aware of the above cultural differences, can expect a lot of problems in their relationships, unless there are some compromises with persons of those cultures. If these differences are submerged by the Ego and he has been dealing with people for years differently you may notice a power struggle between his Ego and his cultural influences.

The main point is that you must have a clear picture of the differences of your spouses or friends' culture as opposed to your own or to what he wants to hold on to.

Let's just look at a few more cultural indifferences noted by Elizabeth Randall-David, Ph.D., page 33; Nonverbal Communication:

Much of what is communicated is not verbalized but conveyed through facial expressions and body movements that are specific to each culture. It is important to understand the cross-cultural variations in order to avoid misunderstandings and unintentional offenses.

Silence. Some cultures are quite comfortable with long periods of silence while others consider it appropriate to speak before the other person has finished talking. Learn about the appropriate use of pauses or interruptions in your "loved ones" culture

Distance. Some cultures are comfortable with close body space, while others are more comfortable at greater distance. In general Anglo-Americans prefer to be about an arm's length away from another person while Hispanics prefer closer proximity and Asians prefer greater distance. Give your "loved one" the choice by inviting him/her to have a seat wherever they like.

Eye contact. Some cultures advise their members to look people straight in the eye (Anglos) while others consider it disrespectful (blacks), a sign of hostility or impoliteness (Asians, Native Americans). Observe your "loved one or friend" when talking and listening to get cues regarding appropriate eye contact.

Emotional Expressiveness. Varies greatly from one culture to Another. Some cultures value stoicism while others encourage open expressions of such emotions as pain, joy, and sorrow. Asian Americans may smile or laugh to mask other emotions.

Body movements take on different meaning depending on the Culture. Some consider finger or foot pointing disrespectful (Asian), while others would consider vigorous handshaking as a sign of aggression (Native American) or gesture of good will (Anglo-American). Observe your "loved one or friends" inter-actions with others to determine what body gestures are ac-ceptable and appropriate in his/her culture. When in doubt, ask.

Here are a few terms that have vital meaning in explaining the cultural dilemma:

A Cultural Group is defined as a people with common origins, customs, and styles of living. The group has a sense of identity and a shared language. Their shared history and experiences shape the group's values, goals, expectations, beliefs, perceptions and behaviors from birth until death.

Racial Minorities is one whose members are readily identified by distinctive physical characteristics that are perceived as different from those of other members of society, such as skin color, hair type, body structure,shape of head, nose or eyes " (Axelson, 1985 (125)

Ethnocentrism is the tendency to view one's own cultural group as the center of everything, the standard against which all others are judged. It assumes that one's own cultural patterns are the correct and best ways of acting.

Cultural Relativity is the idea that any behavior must be judged first in relation to the context of the culture in which it occurs.

Cultural Universal for example, the following structures or functions are found in every extended culture: a family unit, marriage, parental roles, education, health care, forms of work or endeavors to meet basic physiological needs, and forms of self expression that meet psychological and spiritual needs.

Acculturation is a term which is used to describe the degree to which people from a particular cultural group display behavior which is like the more pervasive American norms of behavior. The degree to which people act like mainstream America is related to the amount and kind of exposure to dominant Anglo standards and behaviors. Factors that may lead to a higher degree of acculturation are: 1) a relatively high level of formal education, probably a minimum of several years of high school; 2) birth into a family that has lived in the United States for at least several years; 3) extensive contact with people outside their ethnic and/or family social network; 4) for immigrants, immigration to the U.S. at an early age; 5) urban, as opposed to rural, origin; 6) limited imigration back and forth to the mother country; and, 7) higher soci-economic status. Other factors influencing individual differences are age, sex, occupation, social class, religious affiliation, and family size.

Cultural Values are "standards people use to assess themselves and others...(a cultural values) is a widely held belief about what is worthwhile, desirable, or important for well being: (Schilling and Brannon, 1986, p2)

A Cultural Broker is a mediator between people groups from two cultures.

Even though as an Ego ages, unless he maintains a practice in his culture; his cultural influences may diminish. It is good to be aware of what they were. It can at least tell you how far he has come in adopting other norms. Let's look at Racism and its influence.

Racism has been a deadly germ in the root of many cultures. Therefore, it plays a role in creating conflict. Inter racial relationships have been known to suffer from this sometimes hidden beast. Especially where an Ego has been groomed to believe that his race is superior to another and that certain innate or natural functions one race limits them to performing certain functions in life.

This concept can also cause one person to believe a person is to be treated in certain prescribed ways. Such as the theory of Darwinism, which is terrible when it gets to the view of automatic extentionism.

Racism must be understood, even if your spouse or friend has grown beyond the belief. Your suspicion that he or she may have a touch of it hidden can cause you to misread the Ego's expression.

One example of a misread Ego is when a person may use a racial slur, like "nigger or peck", towards or about ones spouse or friend. Maybe stemming from an altercation. The Ego may not practise using the insultive statement, but may have either allowed it to slip or wanted to hurt the other person's feelings. Whom he knows is against such thoughts and expressions. This, however, doesn't make him a racist.

If the True Ego is a true racist you will really need to help him see the true value of all people. And just like the links in a chain, the chain can't be any stronger than its weakest link. He/she must see this.

Patience and tolerance will be your best tools in dealing with a person who is blinded by racism. He can't see you without the eyes of racism unless he removes it. And to combat it you will need to study the racial indoctrination.

One thing for sure, if a racist is willing to spend some intimate time with you, unless she/he wants to dominate you or feed off of you, she/he has made one step towards putting racism aside. Work with your friend or spouse.

Hereditation seems to produce some personality traits and sometimes an entity may challenge the thought of behaving similar to a relative. Especially, if it interferes with an Ego task he has to carry out. Though some traits are supportive of the Ego, if there's a disagreeable trait the Entity may need help with it or your patience in dealing with the same.

As was pointed out earlier, some families have all doctors, or all lawyers, or all politicians. If the trend is established an Entity must establish whether or not his True Ego calls for him to follow it or to develop other skills. Or he may learn to generalize, like instead of playing professional ball he becomes a professional coach. It's his decision and he must do his own self appraisal. You may be called on to help.

You can, however, spend some time observing your spouse or loved one to see if it appears that the family choice is fulfilling to her/his True Ego. If it doesn't appear that way you may want to ask them how they feel about it. Some Egos follow the family tradition out of respect and responsibility.

If the Ego does follow the family's tradition of say being a minister, and find that his True Ego calls for something else. He can honor their tradition and follow his True Ego. He doesn't necessarily have to be a minister but he can surely start a ministry, hire a minister and still pursue his Ego Goal. Maybe his son may want to be a minister. But for him not to pursue his True Goal may cause the world to miss out on a valuable contribution, a necessary piece of the puzzle.

Religion is another variable that can and does influence the development of the Ego. However, since it can be seen within the culture, race and maybe heredity it could be studied there.

Concepts like superiority, righteousness, and condemnation are thoughts together that carry. According to Fruedians religion is used to help develop the SuperEgo. Therefore, it may be rooted to stay.

Remember that a spouse or friend not practising racism, culturalism, religion, and may have no problems with the role of sex and yet behavior can still emerge in contradiction to the Ego, as you know it. You must be patient enough to allow their influences to rise and fall. Some of their influences can be very positive and some very negative. They still must be dealt with, known and understood by you and your loved ones.

EGOTISM
Human interaction creates a situation
For others to be considered
Therefore, a selfish person is in
Violation of a relationship
Where his desires are the only
Ones sought

****

Love that wants to be served
Is a selfish love

****

It is not a crime to put yourself
First
It may be one to be for yourself
Only

****

To know yourself is an emerald
Divine
To know others is the
Pearl

****

Somehow life by creation
Did make us one
What is it that has made
Us today
Not see it?

****

CHAPTER IX.

EGOTISM

Egotism to the Ego-ologist is like dirt in a sanctuary. It's like a black spot on a white suite. It just doesn't get it.

For one, Ego-ology believes that to be a well balanced Ego a person must give and share. Not only because of a good nature, but because it leaves the door open for others to be willing to help him or her.

In Ego-ology we are teaching a person to help in the development of the Ego. A selfish person would only look beyond the needs of a spouse, friend or child and become engulfed in Egotism. Not that they wouldn't help at all, but in Ego-ology you may sometimes need to spend a lot of time and make sacrifices to help your companion or friend.

There is an illusion of self esteem being imbibed through acts of conceit. But, to be conceited is not the true way to self esteem. It is more of a false air, a facade. It could even mean that the Egotistical person is afraid that the more he engages, shares, or gives to others the less he may end up with to support his Ego.

It is not to say that a person needs to give all that they have to others to duck the Egotism syndrome. But a well balanced Ego needn't fear that he won't be acknowledged unless he hordes every inch of attention for himself.

Egotism doesn't just mean, then, a stingy person, but also one who's prone to disregard even the mere existence of someone else. Especially if it takes away the limelight from himself. And, even though the Egotist is conceited, and you would want an Ego Entity to at least be self concerned, it goes far beyond just viewing oneself in a positive individualistic way.

In Ego-ology our concern is the development of the Ego. But, this is not to be misconstrued with Egotism. We want the Ego Entity to find his True Ego and keep focus on his real goals and the Ego task. But not to look beyond those who are supportive of them and closes to being able to merit their attention and consideration. Once we have encouraged others to help an Ego Entity surely he should be prepared to do likewise.

If your spouse, child, or friend is showing signs of this divisive clutter to the causes of Ego-ology, you have some work to do before this germ takes root. So get busy. Remember that there is a level of awareness where you find that others are a part of you. That oneness removes the idea that you need to be egotistical, unless the whole is being considered.

You could remind them to do unto others as you would have them do unto you. But, we've discovered that a lot of people were measuring what the other person had in their barn before they gave anything (which says that they weren't willing to give any more than they knew the other person was able to give in return).

You may be able to get away with saying, "Do to me as I do to you," too. But, we feel that the best way to instill altruism is by making that a growing principle, rooted while the Entity is young or whenever he starts to formulate the character he wishes to become.

When people do meaningful things for others it's very healthy to true self esteem, which brings us to the word charity.

One good way to foster charity and consideration for others is through seeing people as a part of yourself. See the universality, the brotherhood, of all men. See, the Ego aspect that makes you one with mankind. Of course, there's a saying that "Charity starts at home." So we would say that beyond that charity starts with the Ego Circle.

That Ego circle you have formed to help you be what you want to be is close to you, therefore it should be easier to feel for them and be considerate. You can be more empathetic for those who are like you in varying ways. And, also, supportive of their plight.

You can also as an exemplary trait of the Ego, give to charitable works; such as, Boys Clubs, Big Brothers, Senior Citizen Self help groups, handicap foundations, churches, and the like.

Thus, giving should be a natural fulfillment, from a natural wish. As long as an Ego is being rewarded by his behavior he is subject to repeat it. When a gift you give brings a smile to your face then you know you have accomplished a goal for yourself as well as that person. Giving then can be and feel good to you. Try it. The next time you give a gift to someone, notice how it makes you feel to do so. (don't step to the side and say, "boy, I know I'm going to get paid for giving her this one") Not only are you glad for the person's fulfillment and joy, but for your giving as well.

Some people, however, have been brought up to get all that they can and be concerned about themselves only. If you are concerned about one's Egotism then Ego-ology would suggest that you get to work! You only need to find one person or situation that he may be willing to give to or better sacrifice for and you've found your start.

You can even set yearly charitable goals for your Egotist. But, do remember the aspect of Egotism that deals with false pride. The false Ego is famous for that one. Yet, as long as there are greater persons or lesser ones he should be admonished to keep a level head. Even in giving he must not be conceited nor demanding a return. Nor fix an Ego thing out of it. Like saying " I just gave $100 away mister! If it weren't for my contributions they'd be in big smoke." With that statement Egotism has risen again!

You have to help taper the Ego down. That's closer to the Ego he wants and needs to become. Find a way to tell him that, and yourself.

EGO MANIA

There's an extreme position of the Egotist that is so far off that I started not to mention it. It's called " Ego-Mania." This is a stage of the

Egotist where nothing can be seen and accepted as being greater , more important than or even necessary to consider except that Ego's wishes. This degree of Egotism only sees a person in terms of how he/she can serve them. He wants to be honored, worshiped, admired, and even feared.

Your Ego development, or goal would be irrelevant to one with this extreme form of Egotism, unless your purpose is to serve him.

Some parents have been known to be dictators to their children throughout their lives. They never let up nor allow them to become anything other than what they say. "I" is their favorite word. It's Lucerferic.

The philosophy of one of Egomania is very hard to penetrate unless you can determine its source or cause. It's not mere selfishness but it could be rooted in self preservation or racism, or fear, etc. Or he may simply want to maintain a degree of supremacy or control. Whatever the cause may be it needs to be reached, discovered, and dealt with.

Once you determine what that cause is, you have to do something to balance his fears or to show that what you need to accomplish is too important not to consider certain things. (don't go straight to saying that it's just as important as what he wants. You might really get the boot for that) Use a little finesse when presenting your position. Point out the significance your objectives have to your growth. Show what you have discovered about yourself that needs to be developed. You can also show what could happen if he were not allowed to develop certain ways.

You may have your work cut out for you, though, because Ego maniacs want to control. And regardless of any logic you present if it threatens their control they will be quick to oppose it. They may even ask, "who told you you needed to be this?" "Where did you get this idea from?" "I told you what was important to you." " You couldn't see that?" You don't think I know what I'm talking about?" "Why are you questioning me?"

You may then have to show him why his way couldn't have worked out as good. But you must show that you are sure of yourself. This will be a challenge and you may need to prove yourself. But it's all for the good because the Ego of the Ego maniaist may just be old fashioned and know no other way to handle dealing with you. Or his value system may be founded on principles he's afraid to compromise with) If you can prove your self theory before him he may feel compelled to allow you some room. It would be good then to still ask his advice on personal matters in the new area or of yourself. That way he can still feel he's in charge, until he has grown to the point where it won't make any difference. What you want , then becomes just as important as what he wants. He can't get much out of you if you're not willing to live or are not up to par on yourself.

It is also possible that you can grasp this concept of Egomania if you're not careful when exalting the Ego. Make it a point to be mindful of yourself. You need to keep a level head and see the value in each person. Their purpose is as important as yours and needs to be fulfilled.

Therefore, let us remove from us any sign of over possessiveness and allow others to grow and play down this Ego mania thing that can be so destructive to women and men.

EGO-OLOGY, AGING AND THE AGED

In the Aged we find
What has been, what is
In the youth we find
What is to be

****

Their hands have met
The plow
Their legs have
Stretched the miles
Their hearts have
Bore the woes
The Elderly

****

To experience life
Is more treasured than
Just to live
The difference is in
The knowing and
The unknowing

****

There comes a time in one's life
Where they must determine
What course they must take
At maturity

Then there's another time in one's life
Where they must determine
Again what course to take
At retirement

CHAPTER X

EGO-OLOGY, AGING AND THE AGED

There are many theories on Aging. You can choose whichever one you believe fits the description of your experiences or that of your loved ones or friends. We will start by simply quoting a few of the existing ones according to "Psychology In Action" by Huffman, Vernoy, & Vernoy: page 489 -490:

"There is an Activity Theory of aging that suggests successful adjustment is generated by an active commitment to life."

" The Disengagement Theory of aging states that successful aging involves a natural and mutual withdrawal between the society and an individual (a concept in preparation for death) However, it would be a long stretch if a person retires at 65 and lives to 95."

" It is the developmental psychologist that works to describe, explore, predict and sometimes aim to modify age related behavior. Some theorists propose three different sets of explanations to how we develop and grow. Through nature or nurturing, either continuously or in stages and being stable or changing."

" The Nature aspect or rule suggests that human behavior and development are governed by automatic, genetically predetermined signals called maturation. An example is a flower that blooms in accord with its genetics.

However, on the Nurture side the determinants of development are learning and interaction with the environment.

" Stage Theorists state that development occurs at different rates. Alternating between periods of little change and periods of abrupt rapid change."

Regardless of the theory, aging poses its own unique problems and it's true that our society hasn't been able to develop an image, definite enough, to use, for our Senior Citizens. This group represents people who have already retired or are close to it. They are, for the most part, out of a definite role by which to keep themselves active. And, in most instances, they have been outcasted from the mainstream of society. Their Ego is, more than likely, resting or they have finished their Ego task or goal. How do we help the elderly with Ego-ology?

Being instructors and advisers can be an Ego task undertaken by the Senior Ego's in their latter days. That's if they want to remain that active in life.

There's also another group of Senior Egos who would rather pick up hobbies they may have had or wanted and never pursued. They can engage in those activities as past times or gain extra income from them.

Then there's another group who may need or want a second vocation for their latter years. They may even develop another Ego, a new Ego Circle, different social settings, a whole new Ego world, and experiences to match it all. Especially for those who can afford to get that involved. And, for those who can't afford new activities, because of lack of finances and stamina can join support groups.

There are free activities being sponsored by schools, churches, non profit organizations, the local Office on Aging, Parks and Recreation Centers, and other concerned groups for Senior Citizens.

Looking now at the first group of Senior Egos, (those that can be mentors, teachers, etc.) We see that they can be vital contributors to the growth and development of younger Egos.

Of course, the problem with being paid for their services is the problem of retirement, in the first place. Therefore, unless they work as volunteers, they may not get paid. It is true that some may not need or desire payment, except for, maybe, expenses so that it won't cost them anything to travel, teach, lecture, etc. Even some grants cover out-of-pocket expenses. Some, however, can get paid.

Just remember that yesterday's Egos are the forerunners of today's Egos. In addition to the above, Senior Egos can give advice in making decisions about career choices, business, legal advice, marital and religious advice, etc. They're the experts, builders, innovators, and wisdom of the fields of work. They have inseminated the ideas of our time.

The problem in paying some Senior Egos, again, is also tied up in whether or not they receive government assistance of some sort. To receive funds from the government and from a hiring agency may mean a deduction from the government, along with several other problems.

The second group of Senior Egos deals with those who can develop hobby choices. This could lead to Multiple Egos if he gets too far into it. And it can range from sketching to masterpiece paintings. It could also lead to or become another vehicle to latter day dignity. Some hobbies, especially in the arts, can give the Ego a heightened degree of relaxation.

Barbara Smith and Barbara Sher had the following to say in their book " I Could Do Anything." page (P139):

"...if you're burned out, learning something new or doing something creative is the cure. Plain and simple. It not only begins the healing process immediately by refreshing your mind, it wakes up the imagination you forgot to use. It rests the part of your brain you used too much by waking up the part you hardly used at all."

And the last group, that's similar to the first but may require the development of another Ego, is taking up a second vocation. This may mean the development of a whole host of situations and circumstances congenial to the new vocation or new Ego. Especially if they are still living with relatives.

If they are living alone they will have to (unless they consult with someone else) develop the new Ego alone. If they are in a group home they'll have some assistance getting things together. And if they're in a Nursing home they may have some help, if they are allowed a vocation at all.

M's Smith and Sher made another comment about living again on page 210:

" You can forget until mid-life that only part of you is a provider and a parent; the other half of you is just-you. Inside everyone of us is a unique spirit that belongs only to us. This spirit doesn't bring home wages or take care of anybody and it's completely free to want fantastic things - to run the four-minute mile, or to be a mystic.

...It's not that you should have run your life differently; we all need to take up responsibilities at a certain age, to love and care for people besides ourselves or to build our careers. But one day it's time to give up some of those long-time responsibilities and begin a second life."

" Now, after you've cleared away a lot of the internal debris about your past and present, you'll naturally want to fall in love with a new future.

The thing about you is that you have a great capacity for love of your work. If you loved your first career, you will love another career the way people who loved married a first time love being married again." page (234)

Ego-ology would have you aid in the Senior Egos wish to work, as long as it's physically, mentally, spiritually, and financially possible. Developing the Ego at a late age is not much different from that of an earlier age, except for certain problems like health, maybe speed in recall, etc.

Senior Egos are constantly being stereotyped and sometimes condemned for aging. These minimizing views can be very damaging to the Ego of the Elderly. Some might say, "you are too old to work, " others might say, "you're getting in somebody else's way, you've had your turn."

As long as there are persons vying for a Senior Egos job, status, or the attention he may be receiving, all forms of name calling and criticism will exist. Of course, some of the statements may be true. You might be in somebody's way. You might be "over-the-hill." You may even decide to leave because of it. But, there are other hills. Who's begging? You might get over trying your hand at something else.

Some people actually like to deal with the older worker, especially because they don't anticipate a lot of mistakes being made by them. And they are excellent when it comes to training staff. The only suggestion I would give is to remember the generation, technological, and educational gaps. For new ideas and new Ego Entities have to be known, understood, and used in our modern day Ego tasks. To bridge these gaps, for most Senior Egos, that only means the reading of a few new books to catch up and they're ready to roll again.

There's an organization called A.G.E. Incorporated (Assisting the Growth of Elders) which is a Senior Citizens Self Help program (non-profit) and they look for the Senior Ego to rehire or re-involve into meaningful activity in society., Part of their scheme is to establish the usefulness of Senior Citizens. They consider them jewels to be kept. It is the Philosophy of A.G.E. Incorporated that growth doesn't discontinue at 65) sixty five even though many persons approach this age with an (over-the-hill) attitude and decline from many of their social activities, especially those with little education and in low income sectors of our present class system.

" We believe that there's an appropriate way of growth. Growth involves balance, and because of the lack of social integration the elders may not be receiving the proper ingredients (social interaction) to provide their balance for growth."

They also point out that planners predict that by the year 2025 almost 50% of the American population will be 50 years old and over and that Senior Citizens will represent 22% of the population. They call this the "The Graying of America.": therefore, there's a need, now, to establish a definite role for Senior Citizens.

There are also other groups throughout the country seeking to help and utilize the knowledge and skills of Senior Citizens.

There are groups such as S.C.O.R.E.(Service Corps Of Retired Executives) which is a voluntary, non-profit, non- political organization of Retired Business women and men who draft proposals to submit to the S.B.A. (Small Business Adm.) They also give business advice through workshops and lectures, etc. There are over 12,000 SCORE volunteers serving in all fifty states as well as the District of Columbia and Puerto Rico.

" The purpose of our organization is to serve as a volunteer body of public-spirited citizens by assisting the S.B.A. in its continuing effort to foster the free enterprise system. We aim to help the small business man or woman become a better business person through counseling. This objective is of equal or perhaps greater importance when applied to the prospective new business person, eyeball-to-eyeball advisory relationship."

States have an Office on Aging with area agencies to cover counties. They normally keep a list of various organizations that seek the services of Senior Citizens. Also many non-profit organizations may be looking for volunteer help. Or know where you can be hired.

If you are a loved one, son, daughter, grandchild or other acquaintance and would like to see your Senior Ego active then show it by becoming involved in their development. That Senior Ego may become someone totally alien to you and what you expect. But it's their choice.

Have you ever had a Senior relative that worked hard each day for years? They had no real social life, except maybe around the house. They wore the same kind of construction outfit or nurses dresses for years. Then all of a sudden they retire, fix their hair, put on some slick outfits and start going out to dinners , shows, and a few other places. You see this social glow (and of course you get jealous) and wonder who in the world is this? What's going on Grandma? Grandpa, what's this new look on life? Of course, they just go ahead about their business and don't even put you down.

Though they may appear like a "New You" to you, but that's more of the "Old you being revived." To you it looks like they shouldn't be doing this. You want the same old person who's been giving you all the attention. They lived in their Ego task until the time of retirement. And they may have repressed all other desires and sacrificed their livelihood until that time.

So, you can start assisting them today by probing to find out what it is they may want to get themselves into. May it be a hobby, community service work, or a second vocation. You may have noticed earlier in life something the Ego may have wanted to do, but couldn't find time to or couldn't afford to or maybe they just lost interest. See if they are interested now.

According to Bell, 1989; Bengtson, Kasschau, and Ragan, 1977, Healey, 1986) Elderly men have more social status, income and sexual partnership. However, elderly women have more friends and are more involved in family relationships. Yet have lower status and income.

Those statements to findings can suggest activity that you can expect Senior Egos to be engaged in. Men go out more and meet new people. The social setting may differ but they are being honored and that can work as a reward for attending various engagements. Women, on the other hand, may be limited to the home or community because of a lack of funds. Yet continue to help solidify family relationships and community solidarity.

It is good to encourage the Senior Egos involvement in helping with the development of the younger Egos in the family and the community. If they are spiritual Egos, too, then, maybe they won't mind helping at the Temple, Mosque, or Church.

Senior Egos may not mind going on trips, taking classes like music, art, writing, etc; maybe they can share some experiences by writing a book. It could be a joint project and earn them some extra income. You won't know unless you ask.

You can also get them involved in helping you with your life. Sometimes you can make them a surprise lecturer on some subject she/he can be of help on. You and a few friends just show up at their house with a host of questions and a tape recorder. Of course, if they are busy that night you'll be the first to know it! Just take a rain check.

You can also help them to develop another Ego Circle on an undertaking they may endeavor to engage in. You can form a club and elect them as chairman. It's not hard to find activity, especially if you're looking for it. You just need to do a little research and be inventive. But don't make the mistake of pressing them if you see too much resistance to what it is you are proposing. And, if they'd rather do it alone, let them do so. Always, however, check later to see if they are willing to allow others in on everything.

There was an article published by newsweek on June, 30, 1997 entitled " How To Live to 100." In it Geoffrey Cowley quotes some interesting statistics: pg. 58:

"Life expectancy in the United States has nearly doubled since Angeline Strandal was a kid from 47 years to 76 years. And though centenarians are still rare, they now constitute the fastest growing segment of the U.S. population. Their ranks have increased 16 fold over the past six decades - from 3,700 in 1940 to roughly 61,000 today... The Census Bureau projects that one in nine baby boomers (9 million of the 80 million people born between 1946 and 1964) will survive into their late 90s and that one in 26 (or 3 million) will reach 100."

" The disability rate among people older than 65 has fallen steadily since the early 80s, according to Duke University demographer Kenneth Manton, and a shrinking percentage of seniors are plagued by hypertension, arteriosclerosis, and dementia. Moreover, researchers have found that the oldest of the old often enjoy better health than people in their 70s." also on page 63 we find:

" By the year 2050, the demographers tell us, about 75 million Americans will be 65 or older-twice as many as there are now.":

" Family and living arrangements will be transformed. Because of high divorce rates and longer life spans, more women will live alone. At the age of 65 women outnumber men 5-4, but at 85 the ratio is 5-2. That could be a recipe for more poverty and depression and isolation, especially since older people increasingly want to live independently. Experts predict that more adult children will move in with their parents to counteract the loneliness."

Ego-ology is only one tool by which we can help Senior Citizens prepare for the second life and deal with it. They might end up living 10 to 30 more years after retirement. Doing what? We can work on that together.

THE ID, EGO, AND SUPEREGO

The SuperEgo, an undefinable
Reality that declares itself
By saying " I AM

****

The Ego, a manifested Entity
That declares himself in
Saying " I Am That I Am "

****

The Id, a force of the Ego will
Which says " The I Am Has Sent Men "

****

The faithful has strength
When the strong runs out
For their strength becomes
That of existing power

****

To find the Self
Is to grasp
The jewel of life
To behold thine greater
Self
Is Divine

****

ID, EGO, SUPEREGO

Universe	Super Ego	Super Conscious
External World	Ego	Conscious
Internal World	Id	Subconscious

EGO FUNCTIONS

EGO MANIFESTATION - EGO TRANSFORMATION

|||||||||||||||||||||||||||||||||||||||||||||||||||||||||||||||||||||||||||||||||||||||||

ID------------------------EGO------------------SUPEREGO

(95)

CHAPTER XI

THE ID, EGO, AND SUPEREGO

In the theory of Ego-ology we have borrowed three terms, the Id, Ego, and SuperEgo, to help define what we are. However, our definition of these terms may be slightly different than that of Sigmund Frued's, the distinguished Doctor who coined them. We still hold their fundamental meaning.

In "Living Issues in Philosophy," Titus, Smith, and Nolan, these terms are defined as: (page I76) (Sigmund Frued, 1856-1939): ..."according to Frued, the life energy of a person, or the structure of the personality, is divided into three parts: the Id- the deep subconscious realm of instinct, impulse, and passion; the Ego- the element of individual consciousness that is capable of deliberation and that at times exercises some control over the society that has been called conscious subservient to three masters- the id, the superEgo and a harsh external world of nature- the Ego is forced to recognize its weakness, and it easily develops a sense of guilt and anxiety."

The SuperEgo is being defined as a more of a moral, parental and societal awareness or standard of behavior. The SuperEgo being in the preconscious with the Ego while the Id was in the unconscious.

We are also looking at the levels of awareness that were also coined earlier by Thomas A. Harris, MD. in "Games People Play" We are coinciding these levels of awareness with the Id, Ego and SuperEgo. And the worlds that they belong to or function on. The three levels of Ego awareness are (1) Subconscious (Id), (2) Conscious (Ego), and (3) Superconscious (SuperEgo). The worlds that they belong to are: (1) Internal world, (2) External world and (3) the Universe.

There are many different theories on levels of Consciousness that are not to be misconstrued with the three levels we propose. For instance;

" Consciousness is said to exist in several dimensions or categories known as states of consciousness. Which has been divided into normal, ordinary consciousness (waking states) and alternate, out-of-the ordinary consciousness (drug-induced states, sleep, dreaming, etc.) (Huffman, Vernoy, and Vernoy-Psychology In Action 1994)) "

"Normal states of consciousness called controlled and automatic processing (logoan, 1988; Posner and Snyder, 1975) have been defined as alert and high awareness and control of behavior. Controlled processing is generally done by one undertaking at a time while automatic processing is done with little conscious awareness and simultaneously with other activities."

Carl Jung (1936/1969) believed that man has a personal unconscious and a collective unconscious. The personal unconscious is created from man's experience and the collective unconscious is identical in each person and is inherited. The collective unconscious consists of primitive images and patterns for thought, feeling, and behavior that he called archetypes. An ancestral memory of the human race that gives people cultures, their similarities in religion, art, symbolism, and dream imagery."

Let us focus our attention now on the Id as it is defined in Ego-ology.

THE ID

The Id will be our first consideration. It's the part or energy that people see as the Ego or the Ego Entity. It's a reflective energy more like an image in a mirror. That image will look different if you lean or stand a certain way. Or if light is in the room in certain manners. As you change that light, by degrees or color or shades, so shall the image in the mirror change. Have you ever stood in the mirror in the dark where there is just a speck of light somewhere. You are still there, but what are you seen as?

The Id is what we sometimes see of the Ego manifested on the conscious level. While the ego is on the subconscious(the Ego can hide and allow a false image to dwell in its place) level. It's like a surface reality. Though it has been defined as psychic energy or the part of the mind of the Ego that releases psychic energy. It is also the manifestation of that energy. Thus, it is energy made manifest.

The Id is also what we perceive sometimes as man's behavior. (not necessarily his learnt behavior) Normally learnt behavior comes through cues to the mind and the Ego responds, automatically.

The Id is like a type of soul. But to say so means that the soul can exist on three levels as well. Some do say that there's a soul for the mind (subconscious) , one for the Body (the Id expression on the conscious level) and one for the spirit (superconscious).

The Id can end up as the lost, blind, and false Ego. Even the sick and confused Ego. The Id, when it is expressed on the conscious level, is more of a reactionary force which follows the Ego's request one way and the world's demand another way. For it must respond to the actions it's confronted with. When the Id perceives the external world and must adapt or adjust to the external world, while the Ego sends a different message as its statement, the energy of the Id can become confused. And sends back to the Ego distorted messages . The Ego can adapt these messages as true too unless the SuperEgo intercedes. Or someone in the Ego Circle picks up the confusion and presents it to the Ego.

The Id functions as a sense and it perceives thought, more so, through the energy of the act itself. It works like a sixth sense. Check out the following example.:

Say, for instance, a person visits you following a date that night, your date is smiling, yet somehow they're not in as good of a mood as the smile portrays. The Id will pick this other mood up for it is their Id that shows it.

Now, the Id of the person who perceives another mood can reveal it to his Ego. The Ego will get the message and/or sometimes it will allow the Id to address the situation. (The Id can follow the principle of stimulus/response.)

The Ego may, also, manipulate through the Id. (use psychology is what people will call it) (At this point the Id is what we perceive as the Ego) After it has rationalized, then informed, translated and/or transferred to the Id to play it off and follow the Ego message sent. (The smile) The Id itself may have responded point blank, "What's wrong?" either verbally, telepathically or through sense impressions.

Now the Ego may have reasoned that, (instead of asking is something wrong with you-Id message response to Id message stimulus) " if I could just catch my date up in the present time with a few kisses, this gift, and these nice words, that the former circumstance is lost momentarily."

Let's look at this again. The Ego would respond to the smile. The Id would respond to the sense impression and the SuperEgo would know what her problem was.

Another example of the Id is what is commonly called a defense mechanism. People sense defense mechanisms, like vibes someone picks up. That suggests that the Ego is not to be known because here lies a threatful situation. Or he is not to accept the person before it.

An example of a defense mechanism is, say we have a woman who has been ruthlessly dealt a dirty hand by former lovers. Her Ego begins to distrust men because her Ego through the Id discovered that most men believe in fast love. Or sexual gratification as the goal of a relationship and once fulfilled then he is free to leave the female. She feels betrayed by all her confidence in the lies they told just to reap their rewards. (I say the Ego discovered this thought through the Id because normally the real Ego is self confident and reliant. To her the affair is in her hand and she makes it what it should be)

The Ids shield then becomes avoidance, (The Ego says, "I'm a better woman than that" so she uses non acceptance) for exposure relaxes the Ego into a state of willingness, then trust. A deceitful man will perceive trust as a weakness and will use it to proxy into her emotions or convince her Ego to yield to his game.

I don't think all of the functions of the Id have been explained in any text and our definition may be slightly different than Frueds, but we have expressed our views.

Without the Id the Ego would be as if it was dead. No vibes. Like a monk in a mountain. Still. To quit using the Ego as such, also means to not use the Ego for there is no Ego task. No Ego task is like having no purpose in life. No desire for interaction will one have if the Id has ceased to express the Ego. The Ego has no attachment to the world and starts dwelling in the SuperEgo.   Let's look more now at the Ego.

THE EGO

The Ego we have already discussed in chapter one and have shown its interaction in the world. His tasks and his problems all stem from and feed within the subconscious. Here in the subconscious is retained the memory of all the Egos experiences and impressions sent by the Id from the world and from the SuperConscious mind where the SuperEgo dwells.

In the subconscious mind, man, the Ego, is fixed to deal with the world outside while it is in the world inside. Therefore, the subject of the Ego is the subject of the functions of the subconscious mind, that's where he decides from. He learns how to interact in the world from what he experiences in life. These learnt patterns are then stored. The same holds true for Multiple Egos.

According to Carl Rogers (1902-1987) the most vital aspect of the personality is the self. The self being the "I" or me that one defines himself as. Humanistic psychologist today call this the self concept (Psychology In Action, Huffman, Vernoy, & Vernoy)   In living Issues In Philosophy, Titus, Smith, Nolan pg. 75:

...as the human self consists to use the traditional terms, of the cognitive element- the thinking, reasoning, knowing side; the Affective Element -the feeling, emotional side; and the Conative element - the desiring, striving, and willing side.

In the Way of The Wizard, by Deepak Chopra on page 24 he defines the Ego: " Ego is "I" it is your singular point of view. In innocence this point of view is pure, like a clear lens. But without innocence the Egos focus is extremely distorting.":

Page 48:..."If you look at yourself truly, what are you? A creature of experience that is constantly turning into memories. When you say "I" you are indicating this unique bundle of experiences with its private history that no one else can share."

Deepak Chopra also has a book called "Journey Into Healing" he points out on page 124: "One's inner sense of "Me" is built up of images from the past, all the fears, hopes, wishes, dreams, loves, and disappointments one calls "mine" is still left; The decision maker, the screen, the silent witness."

According to earlier views of classical conditioning John B. Watson Human Personality or behavior was determined by learning. Like other behaviorists he believed that infants were born as a Tabula Rosa. which means Blank Tablet. This theory doesn't account for instinct nor perception, when the SuperEgo seems to come in and gives the Ego child a knowledge man has no way of explaining he has. Then the child learns what to do from day to day. He adds it all to his knowledge base as he grows. His conscious awareness also comes from his interpretation of his encounters as he has learned to perceive and define them.

Since we have spoken on the Ego before we don't have to dwell on it. But we needed to point out how the Ego really sits and how the Ego Image (Ego Entity that functions in the world) isn't exactly the same thing even though the Ego Image represents the True Ego in varying degrees.

We have also shown how the Id is used to reflect the Images of the Ego, plus, how it responds to both internal and external stimuli. Plus the demands of the True Ego. Remember the scenario of the mirror. Now let's look at the Ego as it is related to the SuperEgo.

THE SUPEREGO

The SuperEgo has a broader awareness. This super consciousness can be called a God or Cosmic consciousness. It is like the sea that the river runs into and becomes lost therein. It is his link to the universe.

Deepak Chopra, MD. put it this way in his book "Journey Into Healing": page 125, 126, and 136: "You don't have to do anything to find the self-you have to stop doing anything."

" When you get in touch with the part of yourself that is eternal and unchanging, you have true knowledge of your own immortality, and fear melts away like snow in the summer breeze."

"Human consciousness and Cosmic Consciousness are one...The field dances and waits for us to join it. It constantly folds and refolds itself, like an infinite wool blanket tumbling in a dryer at infinite speed."

The SuperEgo is like the captain of the Ego, knowing its course. Yet the Ego, since it follows, more so, the dictates of his learnt behavior doesn't need to or may fail to look towards the SuperEgo . His learnt behavior can also block him from looking to the SuperEgo.

Man's turning to the SuperEgo is sometimes called enlightenment. The light. This Ego is more like a divine Ego. Not just spiritual, though God awareness, (the Super Conscious) is a divine awareness.

In "Living Issues In Philosophy," Titus, Smith, Nolan, they give an example of the quest for the SuperEgo on pages 62 and 63:

" The aim of all Buddhist endeavors is the extinction of self, the dying out of separate individuality." "It's (the buddhist's) whole point lies in that, since everything in the empirical self is impermanent, unsatisfactory, etc. therefore, it constitutes a false self, none of it can be mine, me, or myself. I must look beyond the Skandhas to find my true and abiding transcendental self."

The SuperEgo never attempts to stray the Ego unless it's heading for a disastrous situation that he has no way of dealing with and which isn't or doesn't constitute an essential experience for the Egos learning. The superEgo then can intervene.

The Ego doesn't function from the SuperEgo either mainly because it gets tied up in the external influences that compel his attention. The outside world is where he concentrates too much. And unless some intervening act, that could come from the SuperEgo, (like an accident, some other casualty or near death experience) takes place the Ego may not take inventory of himself and yield to his higher nature. This happens when the Ego is lost, false, blind, confused or sick. It may not do too much good if the Ego is sick. Unless he lands in a hospital.

The SuperEgo can be misread or misinterpreted to be God, Allah, Jesus Christ, Jehovah, etc. It is not. Some people have claimed to have heard from God in various kinds of revelations, but it wasn't. Their SuperEgo or that one of someone else's could have been communicating.

See, the SuperEgo is the True Image and Likeness of God. And as such it is a God. Yet it isn't the God man prays to. Jesus Christ is an example of one who served his Father God, while he was in a close relationship with his Super Ego. He declared that He and The Father were one. His SuperEgo had merged with God's Ego. Remember that he was the son of man (Ego) and the Son of God (Super Ego).

The SuperEgo wouldn't desire the world. The Buddha was called the enlightened one. He would be considered an Ego who has realized his SuperEgo by first being still. When he practised stillness he was honoring a thought and command that Jehovah stated in Psalms 46:10 "Be Still And Know That I Am God."

When one practices stillness he is seeking to first rely on his Super Consciousness/SuperEgo. That doesn't mean he'll meet Jehovah, Allah or Jesus Christ, but that is where you start. Your SuperEgo and their beings are not the same.

However, to be completely in the Super Conscious mind would require a separation from the world. An example of this you would find in the Prophet Muhammad, when he went to the mountain to yield to the Lord. The Prophet Moses went to the mountain, and Jesus Christ went to the mountain to talk to the Lord.

Even though the mountain is symbolically known as the place of man's SuperEgo, it is also a literal place. So those prophets went to a holy place so that while in their mountain (Super Consciousness) their SuperEgo waited for the God that wanted to reach them or they needed to reach from his holy place and give them some divine revelation.

Once they reached their SuperEgo and dwelt in the SuperConscious mind, such consciousness agreed with God, they knew to do the Will of God. And since they had raised their Ego to the SuperEgo they had no other cause than a divine one, they weren't concerned anymore with gratifying the Ego. Actually their Ego task had changed. Moses was a brick maker, Mohammed was a craftsman/merchant, and Jesus was a carpenter. All of them may have been shepherds too. But once their Ego goal had been reached they began to dwell more in their Spiritual Self until they were given their holy work.

If these Egos hadn't separated themselves from the world and went to their high place, in their SuperEgo, they would have just been in their Ego. The Ego Entity would have been caught up in the world and they would have had to adapt to its circumstances, only.

(104)

Thus, the son of man is the Ego Entity and the son of God is the SuperEgo in the world. But to be a Spiritual man or a religious man doesn't necessarily mean that they carter to God directly. They do serve some purpose as such though.

Let's just look again at the Ego Entity of Jesus Christ. Remember when he said "Father why hast thou forsaken me?" He wasn't in his SuperEgo because of his near death sufferings. For, the SuperEgo is powerful. He responded as one in the world without his supercon-sciousness, which would have known what God was doing.

As for the Spiritual Ego it is more separate than most people. Yet the Religious Ego is more holy than others. One leads to the other, if you are on the upward climb. If you are on that journey you will choose a higher Ego as a guide. One closer to their Super Ego. The safer ones are found in Temples, churches, mosques, monasteries, etc. For they have the Ego task of helping the Ego Entity find their SuperEgo. Which will recognize the God that called them to their order...

When an Ego is called out of the world unto his SuperEgo by an order he normally serves in that religion and helps other Egos make the same transition. These are high callings, even though some take them for granted.

The SuperEgo then is man's Godness. That's as high as he can become God in the physical world. That wouldn't be saying he is the Most High God Jehovah or Allah. Adam, Moses, Mohammed, and Jesus were Gods. (of course sometimes you might see a small g used (god) to say or define them as such) Kings and Rulers were God. Don't get paranoid about the word God because it only means a Superior Being. A father can be called a God of his family because the family looks up to him. Some might consider them false Gods if it causes you to be confused or it interferes with your belief in the one divine God. Under the doctrine of the one God, however, they would not be Gods unless they became one with God like Jesus did.

Out of respect to divinity Jesus, Mohammed, and Moses never declared themselves and never thought to be anything but a messenger of God. They used the power of their own Godness but they were more powerful when they used God's power by stilling the Ego and submitting to it. Once they learned to get out of the way (their Ego) they tapped a divine source of energy.

It does stand to reason that a son of God would be a God. But Adam was too. However, he used his power wrongly by not understanding it and following deceit. (he had to learn from the Tree of life) So man had to find the proper way to dwell in his SuperEgo and before God again. The prophets were sent to prepare for the journey back to God.

The point of this discussion is that once man has finished his work (his Ego Goal) he is free to seek his SuperEgo and dwell there. If he remains that separate from the world he is subject to inherit a zeal to see others sitting close to God. God may touch them and they may take upon themselves another task. We can call this a SuperEgo task or if God instructs the SuperEgo to go to the people he has prepared, you would have a divine task. You, as Harry Joe or Betsy Jane, who worked as a mason and a maid, then retired and started seeking higher goals received from God the understanding of the need for all men and women to become closer to him. Would you say you were doing this or God? If you start preaching for the Lord Jesus Christ or God Allah, how can you be working for yourself? Regardless of how great or powerful you are in your SuperEgo you would have to be working for that God. Harry Joe did his work. Betsy Jane's work got done. Their Ego has been satisfied. But the SuperEgo leads you to a greater awareness. Saying "I and the Father are one" is agreeing with the Father. As if to say " I have to go with what he says."

In his book, " The Way of The Wizard," Deepak Chopra MD. explains on pages 48, 49, and 152: (the word wizard in this title isn't speaking about a real wizard per se but rather the ability to work problems out as if you were a wizard.)

...separation is only an illusion. You appear to be separate from me and from other people because your Ego takes the view that we are all isolated and alone. But I assure you if you set your Ego aside, you would see us all surrounded by one unending field of light, which is awareness. Your every thought is born in a vast ocean of light only to return to it, along with every cell of your body. This field of awareness is everywhere an invisible bridge to all else that exists.

" So there is nothing about you that isn't part of everyone else - except as Ego sees it. Your work is to go beyond Ego and dive into the universal ocean of consciousness." "To have "I" you must also have you or it. The birth of Ego is the birth of duality. It marks the beginning of opposites and thus the beginning of opposition."

Our goal with Ego-ology is not to just find our True Ego and its task but our SuperEgo as well. And to learn how to help ourselves, those of our Ego circle, then those seeking or in need of light. You can join us.

EGO-OLOGY AND THE FUTURE

What lies before us
Is already planted
There should be no problem
Knowing it
For we are the Reapers

What lies ahead
The seeds are ours
To sow
We may not reap it
But we know

****

As we seek solutions
To the crucial unknown
Prepare to do what others can't
We will need a vision
In mind or calculator
We will need faith, hope

****

Have we found ourselves
Past the mask of
Social pretenses?
Where do we find time
For the unveiling?
Who will see but us
The Genuine?

****

CHAPTER XII

EGO-OLOGY AND THE FUTURE

The theory of Ego-ology simply emphasizes that man's True self should find expressions. And as we perambulate through our lives we maintain our focus on what we are and what we are to become.

Ego-ology is a tool that makes us obviate those illusionary ideas that we so boldly take hold of and caution us not to prevaricate our lives to please others or some false image of ourselves.

It encourages us to abnegate those persons, circumstances, and beliefs that make us go astray from our True purpose. As we progress through the webs of life that act to hinder us.

We are to be considerate of others, especially those in our Ego Circle and promote their course in life. And we, also, seek to advance each Ego Entity from their inception to retirement. Then at that time, or anytime we seek attunement without SuperEgo, to transcend the boundaries that shackle us to this world of chained elements.

At any time we have been enlightened we can know even another purpose in life. We can choose to serve others. Then we are not just fulfilling our purpose, but we are made contributors and supporters of the causes of others.

The past and future are the thoughts of time, when there is no time in eternity. So our future is but our projection into life of the moments we believe could be if there be a moment. Would there be a moment if we did not exist for it? Where then did time begin, if not at the beginning of the creation of the earth or heaven? Or the beginning of man or the heavens of the earth or the heavens of man? If you think a little, maybe you can see the answer. Time is between Alpha and Omega.

If you designed a building today and it wasn't built until 100 years from now would the building have existed today? We still have a responsibility to the future we say, draw, think, design today.

As we perceive the uniqueness of each man and the vastness of his being we have always endeavored to reach his meanings in all that he does. To know him at any given time and to keep up with him. To help him reach his goals, fulfill his purpose. For without his, yours may not be met. Plus we sense that your purpose and his become one at some point. Is that the point we all seek to reach?

It is apparent, from what we have discussed throughout this book, that the practice of Ego-ology or some other similar forms of Ego Consciousness, growth, maintenance and modification will be needed in the future. Even in our search for the definition of perfection in man we see that it's more difficult to define because of how the Ego becomes such a diverse Entity. It having so many Entities in one, if need be, and then that one Entity standing in need of a definition.

Then we have the complexities of keeping one distinct behavior alive amongst varying personality differences that have just as much of a concrete separate identity as the core or essence character, being or Ego. This core is like a tree and its branches are other self developments. Or it's like a garden where you find so many kinds of plants. They all must be nurtured appropriately.

And as women and men attempt to be more social, considerate of others, and helpful in being aware of and devoted to their growth and well being, the need to understand Ego problems will increase. Solutions will be needed that may not be written in a book or in a counselor's grasp because of how unique an Ego is and its individual growths and , too, you have many people who just won't consent to taking therapy or informing people of their problems.

To secure a future at all, people will need to weed out Ego developments that are not appropriate or not even belonging to them or their loved ones. But may be mere seed thoughts subliminally grasped and trying to grow. Thus, we will need a constant mirror for each other and ourselves and the kind of patience necessary to listen well, decipher one's meanings, hear constructive criticism, accept direct and/or indirect coaching and watch (staying on top of) one's intentions and goals. We'll need to assess and reassess what we believe as a priority for our lives.

Some children can keep up with their sisters, brothers, and friends as they pursue their personal goals. Some can not.

Sometimes our first thoughts are not our best. Maybe just a fleeting desire not meant to do anymore than spark a craving for something even better. Therefore, an evaluation of thoughts and an assessment of needs must be constantly done   .

Once people begin to look closer at themselves, the school dropout rate will decline, social norms and expectations will change, self-destructive attitudes will vanish, drug and alcohol abuse will diminish, and a more humanistic and self supporting environment will emerge. People will be more eager to see others reaching their True Ego Goals. Realizing this is that person's real self speaking and not some confused, fictitious, false Ego having us blinded and caring for a fraudulent entity. Where we are never knowing the person we're dealing with.

To be oneself represents freedom. To be a lie represents bondage, self deceit, and if you are not who you portray yourself to be then who are you? And who are others walking with?

Religion is a medium by which man has been given definition, so has culture, gender, racism and hereditation. Men and women must apply what's essential for their lives and their interaction with others. You can use whatever ideology you want to live by, and to what degree you want to accept it. Of course, if you are half stepping on, say, living a religious life you may not get too far giving advice to others. Because you will be measured by your performance. I guess that holds true for gender, culture, racism and hereditation as well.

I don't say that to discourage you from helping others and giving advice. Even though you may not always say all that you believe, you should have a helpful answer when needed. The answers you seek that disturb or cause conflict for an Ego lies there in that person's Ego. In his perception, beliefs, misunderstandings and his development, regardless of any external factors.

Ego-ology is a tool and all kinds of therapeutic techniques can be employed in helping persons find themself. I can't suggest that you just grab a group and start to run at each other's minds half cocked. Hints and suggestions you can handle but if you don't want to get too carried away you may want to seek professional help. Maybe hire a therapist to join your Ego Circle or a hypnotist if you need to go that far. There are even a few suggestions in the appendix of this book for some hidden problems.

Remember that Ego-ology also applies to groups and organizations in the sense that they have a definite character and purpose that must be maintained. There is genuine value in being a part of a network of people in a common cause. So much so that in order to maintain its purity of form it becomes an imperative task. It should be cherished by the organizers, Directors and Chairmen to pursue an effort to promote, encourage and even insist that the True Image of their group, organization, fraternity, etc. be maintained by all persons involved.

Many times people lose incentive when working in groups and often enough adverse activity can compete against them in maintaining their True purpose. Other priorities can slip in and have people chasing after different goals. One example is funds needed to finance projects, reach objectives, or just to carry out daily activity. If you didn't raise enough funds at the fund raiser or the walk-a-thon wasn't attended by enough people you have a problem. Of course, that's an easy example. What happens when your personal dynamics director leaves who normally orientates new members. And by the time he's replaced the new members have established their version of how the organization should function.? You can easily end up way off course.

Finding the easiest way to perform certain tasks can cause you to short change the image of an organization or group.

In the future the study and practice of Ego-ology will extend in earnest effort to maintaining the character of groups. That means keeping up with lost sheep and backsliders. And a host of other ideas of revitalization.

We are an entity designed for the endeavor of fostering positive growth. Therefore, that is the future for Ego-ology. An endeavor you can be a part of in some way.

" Our Humble Contribution
Earnest Strivings
Sincere Quest
For Yours
As Well As Ours
That's Friendship"

" From The Womb
To The Casket
From Eternity
To Eternity "

SUGGESTED READING
AND REFERENCES

1. " ADVANCES IN EXPERIMENTAL PSYCHOLOGY
   (Ed. L. Berkowitz - New York Academic Press)

2. " AMERICA'S AGE OLD CRISIS '
   (Stephen - Crystal)

3. " HEALING YOUR HABITS "
   (Joseph J. Luciani, PH. D)

4. " IF I COULD DO ANYTHING "
   (Barbara Smith and Barbara Sher)

5. " INNER CHILD, THE "
   (Dr. H. Paul and Robert Wool)

6. " JOURNEY INTO HEALING "
   (Deepak Chopra, MD)

7. " LIVING ISSUES IN PHILOSOPHY "
   (Titus, Smith, Nolan)

8. " MANAGING HUMAN RESOURCES "
   (Sherman and Bohlander)

9. " MOTIVATION AND PERSONALITY "
   (New York: Harper and Brothers

10. " PSYCHOLOGY IN ACTION "
    (Huffman, Vernoy, and Vernoy)

11. " RECOVERY AT WORK "
    (Carol Cox Smith)

SUGGESTED READING
AND REFERENCES
(Continued)

12.   " STRATEGIES FOR WORKING WITH CULTURALLY
        DIVERSE COMMUNITIES AND CLIENTS "
        (Elizabeth Randall - David, PH. D.)

13.   " WAY OF THE WIZARD, THE "
        (Deepak Chopra, MD)

14.   " I'M OKAY, YOU'RE OKAY "
        (Thomas A. Harris,MD)

15.   " HOW TO LIVE TO 100 " (News Article)
        (Geoffrey Cowley)

16.   " THE HOLY BIBLE "
17.   " THE HOLY QURAN "

'

APPENDIX ONE

The following is a technique called Directed Imagination that can be used as a tool for therapy or to locate and address problemed behavior. Even though the Author Joseph J. Luciani, PH. D uses this technique in his book " Healing Your Habits": to help locate and combat addictive behavior or habits, it can be broadened in its use to address Ego conflict and disturbances.

DIRECTED IMAGINATION

" Directed Imagination is a technique that has evolved into a broad-based program for gaining control over most problems stemming from habit and addiction.

The program encompasses the following key aspects: Directing Imagination, attitudinal preparation, physical preparation, environmental or external preparation, hypnosis, a journal, and establishing a psychological content.

The mistake often made by other approaches or methods is to focus too heavily on only one or two of these components, allowing the neglected aspects to find the back door and sabotage your efforts. It is like spending thousands of dollars to decorate a house, never realizing that structural supports are being insidiously gnawed away by termites in the basement. You do not have to be aware of termites to have your house collapse-unconsciousness in any pursuit invites disaster!

A word I use to describe the preparation required in this program is ":Structuring." Structuring describes the implementation of various techniques and strategies designed to bolster, compensate, or otherwise fill in the gaps that may exist in your character. These gaps represent vulnerabilities, chinks in the armor, where your strength and conviction alone cannot be relied upon to overcome your addiction.

Think of these structural supports as spokes in a bicycle wheel. When all, or even most, of a wheel's spokes are added to the outer rim, the result is an astoundingly rigid and durable product.

Structuring provides a "Braced " attitude, without which you become easy prey to withdrawals, confused thoughts and deceptions. The capacity for anticipation, paired with a restructuring of your attitudes, can be used to help you become psychologically grounded."

The " Insecure Child." It represents a specific way of thinking capable of turning your world upside down. From this perspective nothing can be trusted.

The second character and close cousin to the Insecure Child is the " Spoiled Child." The spoiled Child represents a regressive inability to accept or deal with some aspect of life. The insecure Child's strength lies in the ability to create fear and panic. The spoiled child specialty is manipulation. The Spoiled Child is experienced as a destructive or abusive pattern of thinking that can coerce or intimidate you into continuing your habit.

...whenever your ego becomes compromised by an addiction or habit, it is these characters that become the mental manipulators and, at times, the tormentors of your life. They are adept at intimidation, your tendency is to become overwhelmed. When this happens, you either give up or give in to your destructive patterns.

...one last character I call the " Beast. " The beast is the voice of cravings. Unless your addictive problem will entail withdrawal from a specific substance, you will not get to meet this unsavory character. It is the mental image of the physical discomfort you experience when you stop taking into your body a substance to which your body is accustomed.

...differentiating each character is important because each requires a slightly different response from you. The Beast needs to be tamed. You do not need to negotiate with it, you just need to domesticate it.

...the Spoiled Child, needs to be guided by mature, adult strength....the Insecure Child needs support and encouragement.

...all three characters represent arrested potential. At first you will be instructed to sort out their voices and distinguish them from the voice of your mature ego.

...Directed Imagination is a technique designed to realign your thinking, a good portion of which has been made unconscious by your addictive habits. Whether you look inside and find the Beast, The Spoiled Child, or the Insecure Child, your work remains the same: to identify your regressive or destructive thinking and then clothe these thoughts with appropriate characterization. Once dressed in these colorful mental images, the chaotic and confused thoughts of your addictive behavior will acquire a personality. At this point their destructive intentions will become exposed to the full light of the conscious Ego.

...what is left after your mind has become corrupted is a distortion, a pathetic shred of your True character.

...your sense of security depends on whether your developing ego has the opportunity to experience and feel embraced by a competent, loving adult. Such an adult would have allowed you to be carefree and unconcerned with anything beyond your own natural development. When a child grows up in such an atmosphere, anxiety and insecurity are reduced, if not eliminated. If, on the other hand, you were brought up with inconsistency, conflict, or abuse, then insecurity probably flourished.

...take for example, the parent who, out of "love" never stops taking care of the child, who is learning to handle life. He or she may learn only how to remain a child. This unique type of insecurity can leave an adult fearful of life's responsibilities. Such adults expect to be taken care of and become absolutely hysterical at the notion of being alone.

...all security begins with love. When love is inconsistent, over gearing, or absent, the child becomes more and more compulsive about finding security.

...The Insecure Child is fundamentally the voice of distrust. It is this distrust, this wariness and suspicion of life, that winds up instigating a particular protective reaction. This protection has taken the form of an addiction or obsession.

If the distrust is projected onto your relationships, you may develop a fear of abandonment. This particular fear may prod you into compulsive pursuits: " If I can just accomplish that, then I will be loved.

...Once the Insecure Child is challenged with a healthy, adult perspective on life, she or he can start to build trust in your resources.

(pg 39)...what is called for when you face your Inner Child is a mature, well thought out conviction that life must be lived-not avoided. From this premise you can begin to become less involved in the child/symptoms, seeing them for the first time as emotional manipulations, not current realities. There is no battling, no abusing, only strength.

(pg 38)...This same parent child experience is involved in habitual behavior. The ego becomes like the overwhelmed parent who just cannot tolerate the child's pain. Once this happens, the Inner child is permitted to go on and on with the habit.

Pg 40,41) " The Spoiled Child is a whining, manipulative, bratty kid who has come to dominate your psyche just as an actual spoiled child rules his parents.

Children act this way when they have found the secret to manipulating their parents in such a way that they do manage to get whatever they want. This ability to manipulate was somehow incorporated into your development. This childhood strategy designed to handle your early world has now evolved and become entangled in the difficulties of your adult habit.

One basic difference between the Insecure child and the Spoiled child is that the Insecure manipulates by passively waiting to be rescued, while the Spoiled Child manipulates more actively by using power struggles to coerce. A child becomes spoiled when the parents have, on some crucial level, lost control. This loss of control is usually a result of parental weakness, fear, or inability to face up to and control the child. The parents just do not have the inner strength to take charge.

No matter how spoiled your attitude becomes, it is absolutely essential that you remember that there is a healthy adult aspect to the ego, as well as this spoiled child aspect."

(pg 45) " What you have to do with any of the characters involved in Directed Imagination is to become an actor and act your script, allowing yourself to become caught up in the illusion you create.

...rationalization, a psychological defense mechanism, can be defined as a good reason rather than a real reason for the pleasure of habits. "

(pg 46) "...The insatiable addictive desire of the monster within you is not you...you must separate yourself from that in you which has become so destructive." You, your ego, should never become identified with this intrusive, alien, manipulator that has become a squatter in your life."

(pg 48) " Recent research shows that hospitalized patients who are rewarded by the attention of nurses or doctors for moaning and whining actually report more discomfort and pain than patients who are only responded to whenever they stop complaining and show more self-control.

...when you begin to stand up to whatever is doing the complaining or belly aching within you, you begin to cultivate an attitude that not only will put you in touch with your healthy, mature ego but will also alter your experiences as well.

...try to visualize each character clearly. Close your eyes and develop a physical impression, a photograph of your antagonist.

(pg 76) Take a moment to reflect on the flow of your thoughts. You will discover that your concentration tends to cluster around specific themes or patterns of thoughts. These thought-trans are coupled together in such a way that, like an actual railroad train, you can track the caboose all the way back to its engine simply by recognizing each preceding car in the chain. Consciousness reflects this same linear or sequential thinking. The reason you can find your way back to the "engine " in your thoughts is because conscious thinking follows a basically rational mode of operation (i.e one thought connects to its preceding thought, that connects to its preceding thought, and so on).

...conscious thinking is never without some interference or competition of thoughts. You are always paying selective attention to your world, trying to focus on one aspect of your perceptual field rather than another.

...you are a sensory machine continually processing information, not only from your mind, but also from your internal and external worlds as well.

...when you learn to focus on one specific characterization of your withdrawal experience, you will hear only one voice rather than a cacophony of distractions."

APPENDIX TWO

The definition of Psychotherapy becomes imperative to the practise of Ego-ology, therefore, we will define it and also name several different kinds of therapies. Our definitions will be coming from "Psychology In Action," Huffman, Vernoy and Vernoy. Ego Circles may want to adopt any therapeutic approach they may desire and can create their own. Those that follow are some to choose from:

PSYCHO THERAPY

(pages: 551-552)   A term for various therapeutic techniques to promote adjustment to life and to improve psychological functioning. It includes behavior modification, client centered therapy, family systems therapy, and psychoanalysis. (therapies used by professionals)

Psychotherapy attempts to change disturbed thoughts, disturbed emotions, disturbed behavior, interpersonal and life situation difficulties, and biomedical disturbances.

> DISTURBED THOUGHTS: Troubled individuals typically suffer from some degree of confusion, destructive thought patterns, or blocked understanding of their problems. Therapists work to change these thoughts, provide new ideas or information, or guide the individual toward finding his or her own solutions to problems.

> DISTURBED EMOTIONS: People who seek therapy generally suffer from extreme emotional discomfort. By encouraging free expression of feelings and by providing a warm, supportive environment, therapists help their clients replace feelings such as despair or incompetence with feelings of hope and self-confidence.

> DISTURBED BEHAVIORS: Troubled individuals usually exhibit problem behaviors. Therapists help their clients eliminate troublesome behaviors and guide them toward more effective living.

INTERPERSONAL AND LIFE SITUATION DIFFICULTIES:
Therapists help clients improve their interpersonal relationships
with family, friends, and co-workers. They also help them avoid
or minimize sources of stress in their lives such as job demands
or home and family conflicts.

BIOMEDICAL DISTURBANCES: Troubled individuals sometimes
suffer Biological disruptions that directly cause or contribute to
psychological difficulties. Therapists help relieve these problems
primarily through drugs, and occasionally with electroconvulsive
therapy and/or psychosurgery.

COGNITIVE THERAPY
   When people have irrational beliefs, fail to match reality, their
emotions and behavior become disturbed or they become overly
demanding. Cognitive therapy is applied to realign the individual's
thought processes back to realistic behavior by addressing the
faulty belief system that is assumed on an unexamined level.

HUMANISTIC THERAPY
   Therapy approaches that assist individuals to become creative
and unique persons through affective restructuring (or emotional
readjustment) processes.

CLIENT CENTERED THERAPY
   A type of psychotherapy developed by Carl Rogers that
emphasizes the client's natural tendency to become healthy and
productive, specific techniques include empathy, unconditional
positive regard, and genuineness.

GESTALT THERAPY

A form of therapy originated by Fritz Perls that emphasizes awareness and personal responsibility and adopts a holistic approach, giving equal emphasis to mind and body. Gestalt therapist helps a person find their own meanings for their behavior instead of interpreting for them. They are taught to assume full responsibility for their lives. They will ask what are you aware of right now instead of why?

BEHAVIOR THERAPY

The therapist diagnoses the problem by listing the maladaptive behaviors that occur and the adaptive behaviors that are absent. He uses classical conditioning, and operant conditioning and modeling to decrease the frequency of maladaptive behaviors and to increase the frequency of adaptive behavior.

APPENDIX THREE

There are several different theories of attraction that you can look at and apply in Ego-ology. However, we maintain that like attracts like. Those with similar characteristics and experiences tend to draw to each other seeking empathy and support. The following theories come from Psychology In Action, Huffman, Vernoy, and Vernoy:

THEORIES OF ATTRACTION

REINFORCEMENT THEORY

This theory of attraction results from a positive emotional arousal. We like those who make us feel good and dislike those who make us feel bad.

EQUITY THEORY

The theory that people are highly motivated to seek a fair ratio between benefits and contributions for both members in a relationship.

SOCIAL EXCHANGE THEORY

The theory that people prefer to maximize their costs in their relationships with others.

GAIN - LOSS THEORY

The theory that increased attraction will result when we receive unexpected approval from others and that attraction will decrease if initial liking is lost.

APPENDIX FOUR

The following are theories of motivation as quoted from Psychology In Action, Huffman, Vernoy, and Vernoy. They can be applicable in Ego-ology to give us understanding or keys to motivation once it is determined that an entity lacks motivation:

THEORIES OF MOTIVATION

INCENTIVE THEORY

The theory that motivation results from environmental stimuli that "pull" the organism in certain directions, as opposed to internal needs that drive or "push" the organism in certain directions. (Bolles, 1970, 1975; Pfaffmann, 1982)

INTRINSIC MOTIVATION

The desire to perform an activity for its own sake. The motivation is derived from the satisfaction arising out of the behavior itself.

EXTRINSIC MOTIVATION

The desire to perform an activity because of external rewards or the avoidance of punishment. Motivation is not inherent in the behavior itself.

OPPONENT-PROCESS THEORY

In motivation the theory that one extreme emotional state will be offset by an opposing emotion. This opposite emotional state lasts long after the initial emotion has disappeared. The brain works to restore equilibrium (Piliauen, Callero, and Eevans, 19982; Solomon 1980-82)

APPENDIX FIVE

The following are main categories of mental disorders and their descriptions in DSM-IV (Diagnostic and statistical Manual of Mental Disorders) by A.P:.A. Disfunctionals, illiterates, and persons with mental disorders create or have a different type of problem that has to be considered if a friend, spouse, or family member is the subject. Here we are simply naming the conditions which pose their own unique problems.

1.   Disorder usually first diagnosed in infancy, childhood or early
2. adolescence: mental retardation, bed wetting, etc.

3. Delirium, Dementia, Amnestic and other Cognitive Disorders: problems caused by Alzeimers, HIV(Aids), parkinsons, etc.

4. Mental disorders due to a general medical condition not elsewhere classified: problems caused by physical deterioration of the brain due to disease, drugs, etc.

5. Substance-related Disorders: problems caused by dependence on alcohol, cocaine, tobacco, and so forth.

6. Schizophrenia and other Psychotic Disorders: a group of disorders characterized by major disturbances in perception, language and thought, emotion, and behavior.

7. Mood Disorders: problems associated with severe disturbances of mood, such as depression, mania, or altering episodes of both.

8. Anxiety Disorders: associated with severe anxiety, such as phobias, obsessive-compulsive disorder, and post traumatic stress disorder.

9. Somatoform Disorders: problems related to unusual preoccupation with physical health or from physical symptoms with no physical cause.

10. Factitious Disorders: disorders that the individual adopts to satisfy some economic or psychological need.

11. Dissociative Disorders: disorders in which the normal integration of consciousness, memory, or identity is suddenly and temporarily altered, such as amnesia and multiple personality disorder.

12. Sexual and Gender Identity Disorders: problems related to unsatisfactory sexual activity, finding unusual objects or situations arousing, gender identity problems, and so forth.

13. Eating Disorders: problems related to food, such as anorexia nervosa, bulimia nervosa, and so forth.

14. Sleep Disorders: Serious disturbances of sleep, such as insomnia, sleep terrors, or hypersomnia.

15. Impulse Control Disorders not elsewhere classified: problems related to kleptomania, pathological gambling, dyromina, and so forth.

16. Adjustment Disorders: problems related to specific stressors such as divorce, family discord, economic concerns, and so forth.

17. Personality Disorders: problems related to lifelong behavior patterns such as self centeredness, overdependency, and antisocial behaviors.

18. Other conditions that may be a focus of clinical attention: problems related to physical or sexual abuse, relational problems, occupational problems and so forth.

CONCLUSION

In conclusion let us consider the Ego and how it can turn out naturally so that we can be more careful how we develop and grow.

The Ego of man can be his worst enemy. It can get in its own way. However, there has to be something wrong if this is the case. When the Ego feels threatened he seeks to protect himself. When she feels challenged she defends herself. Sometimes the threat doesn't exist. And when he feels inferior sometimes he seeks to regain his supremacy by belittling others. Yet, he might be supreme and don't recognize it.

The Luciferic influence is the worst of these conditions. Lucifer became blinded to true purpose. If God created everything he has True Purpose. To be different Lucifer went opposite of creation. Opposite simply means error and improper alignment. However, the error became a part of creation by causing acts against the original law. The corollary being his lot in life by disobeying God. This caused the need for proper realignment.

Likewise Adam was willing to accept error for his life by following Eve and the Devil His excuse was " The woman you gave me gave me the fruit and I did eat." He blamed God for his decision to follow error. Thus, the need to be right or proper in alignment with True Purpose is primal. Each man's True Purpose supports God's true purpose.

As Adam (man) erred through disobedience to his True Purpose, so can we by avoiding or deviating from our True Purpose. And as Jesus Christ is the epitome of man submitting to his True Purpose so is the need for every man to do likewise. Thus, to know ourselves and our True Purpose and to pursue our Ego objectives and goals are paramount. If your Ego doesn't get in the way of the development of others (and you cause this intentionally) you would be a bigger person. Then it is fulfilled that, "The greatest among you shall be the servant of all." That is when you see the need of man to fulfill his purpose and seek to help him get there.

This is not a Holy text even though man started off as a Holy entity. He knew no one but God. Each mans' life is unique towards the fulfillment of the True Purpose of life. Thus every man's purpose is necessary and relevant to the whole of creation. If error is caused man is taught to correct it by the act of purpose, through recognizing it and praying about it. However, if that entity does not follow his purpose someone else might have to be born for that fulfillment. Which would cause a delay. Such a delay prolongs error and whatever suffering that comes therefrom. Therefore, I contribute to the idea of supporting man's purpose and his fulfillment. Ego-ology is one such contribution. "A Perception " is an earlier work towards the same end. Hopefully, you will do likewise because that is proper for man. We are in this thing together. We therefore should act like it. Many times we harm the life of others and ourselves unknowingly by not realizing the harm in some of our acts. We need to pay more attention to what we are doing and its effect. We need to recognize that man is evolving and we must do our part through ourselves and our families. It's really all natural to do, however, we are not always doing the natural thing.

Reader's
Comments:_____

_____
_____
_____
_____
_____
_____
_____
_____
_____
_____
_____
_____
_____

_____
Name

_____
Street

_____
City   State   Zip code

YOUR ADDRESS WILL REMAIN CONFIDENTIAL.

Return this form to:

_____
_____
_____